The Blessed Word

Letters from God to You

HELEN TROWER

WestBow
PRESS
A DIVISION OF THOMAS NELSON

WestBow Press books may be ordered through booksellers or by contacting:

WestBow Press
A Division of Thomas Nelson
1663 Liberty Drive
Bloomington, IN 47403
www.westbowpress.com
1-(866) 928-1240

Because of the dynamic nature of the Internet, any web addresses or links contained in this book may have changed since publication and may no longer be valid. The views expressed in this work are solely those of the author and do not necessarily reflect the views of the publisher, and the publisher hereby disclaims any responsibility for them.

Any people depicted in stock imagery provided by Thinkstock are models, and such images are being used for illustrative purposes only.

Certain stock imagery © Thinkstock.

ISBN: 978-1-4497-7306-9 (e)
ISBN: 978-1-4497-7305-2 (sc)

Library of Congress Control Number: 2012920106

Printed in the United States of America

WestBow Press rev. date:11/14/2012

Table of Contents

Chapter One:*I Shall Not Die* 1

Chapter Two:*Pray, Pray, Pray* 5

Chapter Three:*Hope Never Gives Up*...9

Chapter Four:*Do Not Ever Give Up On Life* 13

Chapter Five:*"The Lord is My Light and My Salvation…"* 17

Chapter Six:*Peace As a River*...23

Chapter Seven:*"Be Still and Know That I am God"*....................................27

Chapter Eight:*Overcome Evil with Good* 31

Chapter Nine:*The Blood of Jesus* 37

Chapter Ten:*"Hide Me In Your Heart…"* 41

Chapter Eleven:*Don't Faint*...47

Chapter Twelve:*The Cross* 51

Chapter Thirteen:*"Be Ye Holy, For I Am Holy"*...55

Chapter Fourteen:*A Living Sacrifice* 61

Chapter Fifteen:*The Beauty of Repentance* 67

Chapter Sixteen:*Do Not Be the Only One, But Be One!*..............................73

Chapter Seventeen:*If It is Not a Miracle, God is Not In It* 77

Chapter Eighteen:*You Have Not Resurrected Unless You Are Walking By Faith*.....83

Chapter Nineteen:*Sow! Sow! Sow!* 91

Chapter Twenty:*"Bless the Lord, O My Soul"* 95

Chapter Twenty-One:*"Let Love Be Without Dissimulation"Part I*..........101

Chapter Twenty-Two:*"Let Love Be Without Dissimulation"Part II* 105

Chapter Twenty-Three:*"But Ye Are a Chosen Generation:Part I* 111

Chapter Twenty-Four:*"But Ye Are a Chosen Generation:Part II* 117

Chapter Twenty- Five:*"Rejoice in the Lord Always"*................................123

Chapter Twenty- Six:*"Weeping May Endure for a Night"*.......................129

Chapter Twenty-Seven:*"Deep Calleth Unto Deep"*..................................137

About the Author..143

Chapter One:
I Shall Not Die

There is so much our Heavenly Father has given us for a marvelous victorious life in Jesus Christ. Jesus Christ declares that "we should have an abundant life" (John 10:10). As Christians we often have disappointments and discouragements to the point of feeling overwhelmed or unaccomplished. Therefore we are unable to complete the task in which our heavenly Father, through Jesus Christ has assigned us.

There is a great work that needs to be done. God is winding things up quickly. We must never forget our primary being. Jesus Christ did not give us salvation in exchange for pain, suffering and uncertainty, but to bring us into perfect relationship with our Heavenly Father. We are to help others to know Jesus Christ and our Heavenly Father as we do. How glorious our comforter and helper, the Holy Spirit, is to guide and help us in these areas. Many of God's children are spiritually dying. Some of us are losing hope, having despair, and what reality we have is very grim. However, this is not the will of God! God has a special word for you. God knows about being spiritually dead. God knows this can happen to anyone. God loves you and wants you to be set free!

David said it perfectly, "I shall not die, but live, and declare the words of the Lord," (Ps. 118:17). David knew about dying. To die doesn't just mean physical death. Here, David is talking about spiritual death. Death is defined: to stop living; become dead; to suffer agony of death; to crease existing; to stop functioning; to lose force or activity; to become weak, faint; unimportant; to fade away or wither away; to become alien or indifferent; to pine away as with desire; suffer spiritual death. There are the many forms of spiritual death among God's children. It is also spiritual bondage and it torments and is very unproductive. We all have fit in one of these categories one time or another, not knowing or understanding what has happened.

David continued saying "... but live and declare the works of the Lord." Live is defined as, "having life, not dead; having positive qualities; warmth, vigor, brightness; to last; to endure." David said if you don't die, but live, then we will be able to declare the works of the Lord. And then we can become fruitful and productive. The very next verse declares, "The Lord hath chastened me sore: but he hath not given me over unto death" (Ps. 118:19). God knows we have been through a lot of valleys and confronting mountains. But some of it we have brought on ourselves. We make our own decisions. Sometimes we choose God, other times we choose sin. God has nothing to do with sin, except cleanse it with the *blood* of Jesus Christ. And granting us with his goodness that leadeth to repentance (Rom. 2:4).God chasten those that he loves. "As many as I love, I rebuke and chasten: be zealous therefore, and repent" (Rev. 3:19). God chasten David to the point of being sore. Many of us can testify to this with our earthly parents. Punishment, discipline to the point of being sore. We shall never forget those days. They have made us who we are and we survived. This is how it is with our Heavenly Father. He chasten us until we are sore, but he hath not given us over unto death. You are not dead. "As unknown yet, and yet well known; as dying, and, behold, we live; as chastened, and not killed," (II Cor. 6:9). No matter how you are feeling, you are not dead!

Speak this with your tongue. For the tongue is wholesome "healing". "A wholesome tongue is a tree of life; but perverseness therein is a breach in the spirit" (Prov. 15:4). You can speak with your tongue life so you can live. God is granting you that power right now with your tongue. "Death and life are in the power of the tongue: and they that love it shall eat the fruit thereof" (Prov. 18:21). You have the power to speak life into existence right now! Open your mouth and repeat after us, IN THE NAME OF JESUS CHRIST, I SHALL NOT DIE, BUT LIVE, I SHALL NOT DIE, BUT LIVE, I SHALL NOT DIE, BUT LIVE AND DECLARE THE WORKS OF THE LORD!!! Amen.

Chapter Two:
Pray, Pray, Pray

We as a people are in inclined to pray for our families, churches, friends and communities. The Holy Spirit teaches us to even pray for other nations. God wants us to pray for Jerusalem. "Pray for the peace of Jerusalem: they shall prosper that love thee" (Ps.122:6). It is virtually impossible to pray for some of these situations without the help of the Holy Spirit. Jerusalem especially, because of the fact that most of us do not know anyone that resides there or any other nations. Without the guidance of the Holy Spirit our hearts will not turn that way. We would have to love beyond what we can see or feel. "This love is shed abroad and our hearts by the Holy Ghost which is given unto us" (Rom. 5:5). God loves all nations, because he is the creator of all things.

We produce and breed our own families. It comes so natural for us to pray for them. Most of us love our families, churches and friends. Therefore prayer seems effortless. Did you notice that the Holy Spirit said "our"? The word 'our' is a sense of ownership. God knows it is difficult to pray for certain matters without being lead by his spirit. "For as many as are led by the Spirit of God, they are the sons of God" (Rom. 8:14). Ask God to fill you with his Holy Spirit. It is yours to ask for. Do not be a skeptic. God promised it to you. " And it shall come to pass afterward, that I will pour out my spirit upon all flesh; and your sons and your daughters shall prophesy, your old men shall dream dreams, your young men shall see visions:" (Joel 2:28-29).

Prayer is a powerful tool used in the Christian lives. Without it we tend to feel alienated or deprived of God's blessings. The word pray is defined; to recite a "prayer"; to bring about; to get etc by prayer; to ask earnestly; to make supplications to; to worship God by reciting set formulas. God wants you to pray for our nations, churches and families.

There will also be people around us who do not know the word of prayer. They do not have a relationship with God. However this makes it difficult for them to communicate with God. Nevertheless, God still loves them. We are to discern these things and pray for them. This is called intercessory prayer. If we fail to pray for the unsaved, or whom God has placed on our hearts, we risk the chance of being in a sinful state. Samuel knew this when he declared, "For the Lord will not forsake his people for his great name's sake: because it hath pleased the Lord to make you his people. Moreover as for me, God forbid that I should sin against the Lord in ceasing to pray for you but I will teach you the good and right way" (I Sam. 12:23-24).

God wants us to grow to mature Christians. One of the areas we lack is praying for ourselves. Some Christians have not excelled in this area. This is the area we tend to feel uncomfortable in. We are so willing to pray for others but we forget to pray for ourselves. Why? The enemy would have you to believe that prayer for yourself is vain, self-glory and unrewarding. This is another lie that is told to Christians. If we start to pray for ourselves we become strong and courageous in Christ Jesus. Then we would see the results of how God has blessed us and we become excited to pray for others. There are times when we need prayer, we are so trodden we can barely utter, "Thank you Jesus". All prayer must be done with supplication and thanksgiving, for this is the will of God. We have to be thankful. It does not matter what you have to pray about. It can be momentous or minute. In order for the Almighty God to grant us our desire we have to thank God for even listening to our petitions. We must be thankful even in the worse situations. God wants to mold some of us to become a beautiful vessel of honor. "Giving thanks always for all things unto God and the Father in the name of our Lord Jesus Christ;" (Eph. 5:20).

King David knew the secret on how to personally get blessed through prayer. David said, "Look thou upon me, and be merciful unto me, as thou usest to do unto those that love thy name" (Ps. 119:132). David goes further to say in another passage, "Give ear to my words, O Lord consider my meditation. "Hearken unto the voice of my cry, my King, and my God: for unto thee will I pray" (Ps. 5:1-2). Did you take notice how David referred to himself six times in one passage? This is the type of diligence we have to have when we pray for ourselves, in the presence of a Holy God. Do not be timid about this form of prayer. God honors this type of prayer. David knew exactly how to get God's attention. When David was in distress he never submitted to the problem or rolled in self-pity. He was determined for God to bless him through prayer. "Hear my prayer, O Lord, and let my cry come unto thee. Hide not thy face from me in the day when I am in trouble; incline thine ear unto me: in the day when I call answer me speedily" (Ps. 102:1-2). The results of David's prayers being received was, "I LOVE the Lord, because he hath heard my voice and my supplications. Because he hath inclined his ear unto me, therefore will I call upon him as long as I live" (Ps. 116:1-2). Beloved, learn how to pray for yourselves. The results are miraculous!!!

Jesus prayed a wonderful prayer to our Heavenly Father for the disciples and for the ones that shall believe on him. In one of the verses, Jesus prayed for himself "And now, O Father, glorify thou me with thine own self with the glory which I had with thee before the world was" (John 17:5). Three times Jesus prayed for himself at the garden of Gethsemane (Mark 14:32-42). There will be times when we are going to feel compelled to pray for ourselves. This should be done without guilt or insecurities. This time with God is usually alone. The Holy Spirit will let you know when the time is at hand. "Likewise the Spirit also helpeth our infirmities: for we know not what we should pray for as we ought: but the spirit itself maketh intercession for us with groanings which cannot be uttered" (Rom 8:26). THANK GOD FOR JESUS CHRIST OUR LORD AND SAVIOR AND WONDERFUL REDEEMER. "AND he spake a parable unto them to this end, that men ought always to pray, and not to faint ;"(Luke 18:1). Amen.

Chapter Three:
Hope Never Gives Up

❧

Many of God's people are falling short of spiritual blessings. Our Heavenly Father wants to bless his people beyond what we can imagine. All spiritual blessings come from heaven. God distributes the spiritual blessings according to how he has chosen us in him. Paul said it wonderfully, "Blessed *be* the God and Father of our Lord Jesus Christ, who hath blessed us with all spiritual blessings and heavenly *places* in Christ: According as he hath chosen us in him before the foundation of the world, we should be holy and without blame before him in love:" (Eph. 1:3, 4).

As we wait for our spiritual blessings we can become uncomfortable, frustrated and often times feel a sense of lost hope. Being all that God has called us to be is a life time achievement. Many emotions will come to surface during this time. These feelings will come and go. The Holy Spirit wants us to take heed to hope. Hope is a feeling you should never be without. Pay close attention to this particular emotion. A lot of emotions we experience are stirred up through our own anxieties and inferiorities. But hope is a feeling or emotion that was given to us from our Heavenly Father. Hope is defined a feeling, that what is wanted will happen; desire accompanied by expectations; the thing that one has a hope for; to want and expect; to trust or rely; to continue having hope though it seems baseless. We must never believe the enemy when he tells us we don't have hope. God has given every Christian a promise of not just hope but good hope. "Now our Lord Jesus Christ himself, and God, even our Father, which hath loved *us*, and hath given us everlasting consolation and good hope through grace," (II Thess. 2:16).

How Glorious, David knew the significance of hope. David knew that God had given us hope even in our youth, as infants. David declared, "But thou *art* he that took me out of the womb:

thou didst make me hope *when* I was upon my mother's breast," (Ps. 22:9). This is all so wonderful how our Heavenly Father provided and gave us hope at such an early age. Why was hope given to us so soon? Paul declares, "For we are saved by hope: but hope that is seen is not hope: for what a man seeth, why doeth he yet hope for? But if we hope for that we see not, *then* do we with patience wait for *it*," (Rom. 8:24, 25). God knew we would never be able to receive salvation unless we have hope. Salvation is something you cannot see. Therefore, we have to hope for it. And hope is something we cannot see, but we wait for it as unto our salvation.

There are times we may believe that the hope we have is of no use, to the point of feeling hopeless. Contrary to the belief, our hope is very much alive and vibrant. Peter said, " Blessed be the God and Father of our Lord Jesus Christ which according to his abundant mercy hath begotten us again unto a lively hope by the resurrection of Jesus Christ from the dead," (I Pet. 1:3). Jesus Christ resurrected from the dead to live forever and to never die again. Because of his resurrection, our hope will live forever and never die.

We all feel discouraged at times as we wait and hope for our spiritual blessings. Do not just focus on this present life. But focus also on the everlasting life with our Lord and Savior Jesus Christ. When we ponder on falling asleep (or dying) we must still have hope in Jesus Christ for our eternal salvation. If we don't, we will be lacking joy and fulfillment. Paul said, "If in this life only we have hope in Christ, we are of all men most miserable" (I Cor. 15:19). We cannot believe that this life is all God has to offer. We must never limit God's blessings. When we do we become most miserable, as Paul stated.

Beloved, never give up on hope. It assures you of your spiritual blessings and your salvation. There are times you may feel you have lost hope. But this is another deception. You can never lose hope. Hope was given to you at birth. Be strengthened and encouraged and always remember whom you serve, the most High God of heaven and earth. And never forget what Jesus Christ has done for you!!! "I have set the Lord always before me: because *he is* my right hand, I shall not be moved. Therefore my heart is glad and my glory rejoiceth: my flesh also shall rest in hope" (Ps. 16:8, 9).

Embrace this precious hope! It is so wonderful. You don't have to look for it or pray for it. It lives in you. Hope will make your walk with the Lord hand in hand. HOPE NEVER GIVES UP, HOPE NEVER GIVES UP, HOPE NEVER GIVES UP, even to the end!!! "Wherefore gird up the loins of your mind, be sober, and hope to the end for the grace that is to be brought unto you at the revelation of Jesus Christ;" (I Pet. 1:13). Amen.

Chapter Four:
Do Not Ever Give Up On Life

❧

There are times Christians begin to doubt their very existence. This is very common when life seems challenging, or the people we love become ill or their lives are ended. God is not taking life away purposely. Our Heavenly Father gave us life to enjoy. God loves you; don't ever believe he wants to cause you grief or abandonment. God yearns to have an intimate relationship with his people. So much that we have the right to call him Abba, (Abram for Father). This name is only used by God's children for a closeness of unity. "For ye have not received the spirit of bondage again to fear; but ye have received the Spirit of adoption, whereby we cry, Abba, Father. The Spirit itself beareth witness with our spirit, that we are the children of God:" (Rom. 8: 15-16).

God chasten us because he loves us so much. God so desire for you to have a wonderful, prosperous life in Jesus Christ. David declared; "For his anger *endureth but* a moment; in his favor *is* life: weeping may endure for a night, but joy *cometh* in the morning" (Ps. 30:5). God favors life! The enemy would have you to believe the opposite. With wars and rumors of wars, the saints can become disillusioned about life. Oh how wonderful for our Heavenly Father to favor life. Favor is defined; approving; supporting; endorsing; to the advantage of; good will; favoritism. This is how God views life. Life is so precious to God, after all He created it. "And the Lord God formed man *of* the dust of the ground, and breathed into his nostrils the breath of life; and man became a living soul" (Gen. 2:7).

David declares, "What man *is he that* desireth life, *and* loveth *many* days, that he may see good?" (Ps. 34:12). David is saying if you desire your life and love your days goodness will be in your life. David also declares, "For with thee *is* the fountain of life: in thy light shall we see light" (Ps. 36:9). How glorious it is for God to pour life into us as a fountain that flows like a stream. Jesus Christ came for this very purpose "... I am come that they might have life, and that they might have *it* more abundantly" (John 10:10). Jesus speaks of an abundant life; David speaks of a fountain of life. These two are quite similar. The reason why Jesus said, "I came that you might have life is because of the life that is in Jesus. We as Christians don't ever have to walk in darkness. "In him was life; and the life was the light of men" (John 1:4). We should never have darkness in our life. "... I am the light of the world: he that followeth me shall not walk in darkness, but shall have the light of life" (John 8:12).

Jesus declared that he came that we might have a more abundant life. Abundant is defined; as very plentiful; more than sufficient; ample; well supplied; rich. This abundant life that Jesus is talking about here isn't the present life we live now. This is the everlasting life with our Heavenly Father. Jesus didn't just come for this present, short termed life we are living, but also for our everlasting life. "For so entrance shall be ministered unto you abundantly into the everlasting kingdom of our Lord and Savior Jesus Christ" (II Pet. 1:11). Because of Jesus, the life that we have isn't in darkness. And it doesn't end here. We get to have more life when we fall asleep (die). This is the abundant life that Jesus is talking about. The abundant life is our eternal salvation. "And this is the record that God hath given to us eternal life, and this life is in his Son" (I John 5:11).

"Jesus said unto her, I am the resurrection, and the life: he that believeth in me, though he were dead, yet shall he live; And whosoever liveth and believeth in me shall never die: Believest thou this?" (John 11:25 -26). Jesus proposed this question to Martha after her brother, Lazarus, had died. The Holy Spirit is asking you the same question right now. Do you believe that because of Jesus Christ your life will never cease even when you die? Do you believe that because of your faith in Jesus Christ this allows you to have everlasting life? We know you have said yes to these questions. This is why we hold this promised word so dear to our hearts. "For God so loved the world, that he gave his only begotten Son, that whosoever believeth in him, should not perish, but have everlasting life" (John 3:16). Words for our soul. "I have longed for thy salvation, O Lord; and thy law *is* my delight. Let my soul live, and it shall praise thee; and let thy judgments help me" (Ps. 119: 174-175).

Do not ever give up on life. Do not ever believe your life is short termed. And do not ever believe God wants to take your life away. "Verily, verily, I say unto you, He that heareth my word, and believeth on him that sent me, hath everlasting life, and shall not come into condemnation; but is passed from death unto life" (John 5:24). Amen.

Chapter Five:
"The Lord is My Light and My Salvation..."

In times like this, we have an opponent that creeps into our lives to destroy the foundation of what God has given us. It creeps in because it knows it's not wanted. And once it is reproved or exposed by the truth it can no longer stay. It remains in many saints, because it is hidden. The darkness is what covers and conceals it. It only reveals itself when the occasion calls for it. But light will reveal it, and once it is revealed, it must leave. This opponent, no doubt, is fear.

Fear is defined; a feeling of anxiety and agitation caused by the presence or nearness of danger; evil; pain; to be afraid of; dread; to expect with misgiving. Fear is designed to torment and confuse and eventually causing you not to trust God, but trust fear itself. Once you trust in fear, then you will start to feel oppressed. Oppression causes you to feel weigh down or worried, troubled, feeling physical or emotional distress. David said, "Trust not in oppressions..." (Ps. 62:10).

We will always have danger and terror in this world as ominous as they are, they don't give us fear. Fear usually comes when we hear of disasters or terrors are coming or when they are presented to us. Fear is a reaction to these circumstances. Our Heavenly Father does not want you to react to these situations with fear. Once you do not react or respond to the circumstances with fear then there is dominion. Our Heavenly Father wants you to respond with power, love and a sound mind. These were given to you to defeat and tear down what God never gave you, which is fear. "For God hath not given us the spirit of fear; but of power, and of love, and of a sound mind (II Tim. 1:7).

We know that fear hides in darkness and only the light can reveal it. David declared, "For thou wilt light my candle: the Lord my God will enlighten my darkness (Ps. 18:28). Ask God to light your candle, ask him and he will. And what is lurking in the darkness can no longer hide. Once darkness has been enlightened, fear must leave. Enlighten is defined; to reveal truths; to free you from ignorance, prejudice or superstition; to give clarification. Isaiah prophesied about this light. "The people that walk in darkness have seen a great light: they that dwell in the land of the shadow of death, upon them hath the light shine" (Is. 9:2). This light that Isaiah prophesied about is Jesus Christ. Jesus himself declared, "As long as I am in the world, I am the light of the world" (John 9:5). Immediately after this powerful declaration, a blind man, from birth was healed by our Lord and Savior Jesus Christ. Read John 9: 1-41. And witness the healing power of Jesus Christ. Fear and any other darkness cannot say where there's light.

Jesus is no longer on Earth. His work is finished. Jesus Christ ascended to heaven to be with our Heavenly Father. But we are believers of Jesus Christ. Therefore the light lives in us. Jesus proclaimed, "While ye have light, believe in the light, that ye may be the children of light..." (John 12:36). Jesus also declared, "Ye are the light of the world. A city that is set on a hill cannot be hid" (Matt. 5:14). This is what we look like to the world, a city that is sitting on top of a hill. A city on a hill can never be hidden or overlooked. To the world we are magnified. Use this light that we as children of God have inherited through our Lord Jesus Christ. Do not hide this light, it breaks yokes and set the captives free wherever it shines in you or anyone that this light reflects on. Jesus also said, " Neither do men light a candle, and put it under a bushel, but on a candlestick; and it giveth light unto all that are in the house" (Matt. 5:15). Everyone in your house will be healed and set free from darkness! Everyone on your job will be healed and set free from darkness! Everyone in your church will be healed and set free from darkness! Fear and other ungodly spirits must go! Once the light has shine upon the darkness, the darkness becomes confused and it cannot understand the light. "And the light shineth in darkness; and the darkness comprehended it not" (John 1:5). Fear has no grounds where you are because you are the light of the world. Although fear has gripped your heart, it has no reign because of the light of Jesus Christ that lives in you.

David knew this when he declared, "The Lord *is* my light and my salvation; whom shall I fear? the Lord *is* the strength of my life; of whom shall I be afraid?" (Ps. 27:1) Saints, because of Jesus Christ, we have nothing to fear. David continued to say, "Though a host should encamp against me, my heart shall not fear; though war should rise against me, in this *will* I be confident" (Ps. 27:3). David is confident that no matter what, including wars, his heart will not fear because the Lord is his light, whom shall he fear? The Holy Spirit is saying don't let fear stop you from what God has ordained you to do. Do not let this fear move you in any way. " Therefore, my beloved brethren, be ye steadfast, unmovable, always abounding in the work of the Lord, forasmuch as ye know that your labor is not in vain in the Lord" (I Cor. 15:58).

Being that every born again Christian has the light of Christ in them, therefore Jesus presence avails. Jesus is always present with you. Because of Jesus presence, the spirit of fear, and other darkness, will perish at his rebuke. "*It is* burned with fire, *it is* cut down: they perish at the rebuke of thy countenance" (Ps. 80:16). The rebuke of Jesus and his presence alone can reprove fear and can cause sickness and diseases to be cut down and burned up as fire. Luke talks about the divine presence and power of Jesus Christ. "And he arose out of the synagogue and entered into Simon's house. And Simon's wife's mother was taken with a great fever; and they besought him for her. And he stood over her, and rebuked the fever; and it left her: and immediately she arose and ministered unto them" (Luke 4: 38-39). When Jesus stood over Simon's mother in law, just his presence alone, and his rebuke caused the fever to leave.

When Jesus shows up, there is no need for fanaticism. With one rebuke from Jesus the Holy Spirit causes all darkness to perish. That's power! "But ye shall receive power, after that the Holy Ghost is come upon you..." (Acts 1:8). **In the name of Jesus Christ**, we rebuke the spirit of fear in God's people. We command the spirit of fear to go! Fear must leave where there is light in **Jesus name!** "But all things that are reproved are made manifest by the light: for whatsoever doth make manifest is light" (Eph. 5:13). We thank God for your deliverance and that you will continue to let your light shine.   "Giving thanks unto the Father, which hath made us meet to be partakers of the inheritance of the saints in light. Who hath delivered us from the power of darkness, and hath translated *us* into the kingdom of his dear Son" (Col. 1:12-13). Amen.

Chapter Six:
Peace As a River

❦

"O that thou hadst hearkened to my commandments! then had thy peace been as a river, and thy righteousness as the waves of the sea" (Is. 48:18). How wonderful it is to know if we keep God's commandments, we can have peace as a river. So many of God's people yearn for peace. Our heavenly Father wants you to have this peace. Peace isn't something you visualize and possess, nor is it anything that you desire and is granted. The secret to peace is loving and keeping God's law. "Great peace have they which love thy law: and nothing shall offend them" (Ps.119:165). Your peace will be great if you love the law (the word). And amazingly you will never be offended or stumble.

THERE IS POWER IN PEACE! Many of God's people believe that to be in a peaceful state, you have to become weak or submissive. This is another deception from the enemy. There can be no contention or bitterness if peace is to prevail, but this doesn't mean that you are inferior. Many of God's people believe that the works of the flesh their our only protection. This seems realistic to the old man, but that man is crucified and buried with Jesus Christ. "Knowing this, that our old man is crucified with *him...*" (Rom. 6:6). We took on a newness in Christ and the old man has passed away. "Therefore if any man *be* in Christ, *he* is a new creature: old things are passed away; behold all things are become new" (II Cor. 5:17). We have a new way of fighting our battles, a new way of how we view danger. This new way is the antidote that Jesus use. This formula is peace. Peace is defined; freedom from public disturbance or disorder; freedom from disagreements or quarrels; harmony; concord; an undisturbed state of mind; absence of mental conflict; calm, quiet; tranquility.

When you have peace, you are never disturbed, no matter what the obstacles are. When you have peace, chaos and turmoil are nonexistent. Accusations and violations crumble at the presence of peace. Jesus never contended or quarreled with anyone because of the peace that abode in him. There wasn't anything that moved Jesus. God wants us to be the same. When you have peace you are liberated from all disturbance. Nothing in this world can affect you. Your state of mind is calm and tranquil at all times. THERE IS POWER IN PEACE! After all, this peace comes from God. Peace is one of the fruit of the Spirit, therefore this peace is the Spirit of God.

This is one of the keys to a blessed victorious life in Jesus Christ. Jesus always knew this secret. This is why Jesus always blessed the disciples with peace. Jesus also left peace with us before he ascended to be with our heavenly Father. " But the comforter, *which* is the Holy Ghost, whom the Father will send in my name, he shall teach you all things and bring all things to your remembrance, whatsoever I have said unto you. Peace I leave with you, my peace I give unto you: not as the world giveth, give I unto you. Let not your heart be troubled, neither let it be afraid (John 14:26-27). What a glorious promise this is. The peace that Jesus left with us is the Holy Spirit. Peace is one of the characteristics of God. This is why Jesus said, "...let not your heart be troubled, neither let it be afraid", because he knew that it's impossible for us to be troubled or afraid if the us to let peace rule in our hearts.

Many of God's people do not realize what or whom peace is. This is why the Paul declared " And let the peace of God rule in your hearts, to the which also ye are called in one body; and be ye thankful" (Col. 3:15). Paul knew if peace ruled in our hearts nothing could harm us. But Paul was careful to instruct us to let peace rule in our hearts. Rule is defined; to have authority over; govern; direct, to be the most important element; dominate. There are nine fruit of the Spirit, but peace is to rule (dominate). If we grasp this concept then there is victory. THERE IS POWER IN PEACE!

Mark talks about Jesus miraculous encounter with opposition. " And he arose, and rebuked the wind, and said unto the sea, Peace, be still. And the wind ceased, and there was a great calm (Mark 4:39). This is the power of peace. That the glorious affect of peace can cause the raging winds and sea to be still. THERE IS POWER IN PEACE! Nothing can harm you once it's obtain.

Once we have the knowledge of its power all oppositions are ineffective.

This is why God promise in Isaiah 48:18, if we listen to his word and keep it, our peace will be as a river. If you are obedient to God's word, than the Holy Spirit will flow through you, leaving a lingering peace. This is why David stated, "Pray for the peace of Jerusalem: they shall prosper that love thee" (Ps. 122:6). If we are obedient to this word and keep God's commandment Isaiah promise we will have peace as a river.

David knew this. That is why he stated in the next verse, "Peace be within thy walls *and* prosperity within thy palaces. For my brethren and companions' sakes, I will now say, Peace *be* within thee." (Ps. 122:7-8). What David is saying, if you pray for the peace of Jerusalem and pray for his brethren and companions, his people; if you hearken to God's commandment, (his word), in return you will have peace as a river. Then Isaiah 48:18 will be fulfilled. This is a glorious promise saints. Hearken to God's word then your peace will be as a river.

We know that you will have the peace of God dwelling in you. You have yearned for it so long and God knows your heart. In many circumstances peace has already abode, but you are unaware of its presence and power. God wants every saint to have this peace. Father God, we pray that you will grant your people peace... and that you will fill every void with Jesus... and that your peace will rule in every heart... and that the peace of God will flow through every vessel as a river. In Jesus name we pray. "And the peace of God, which passeth all under-standing, shall keep your hearts and minds through Christ Jesus" (Phil. 4:7). Amen

Chapter Seven:
"Be Still and Know That I am God"

❦

"Be still, and know that I *am* God: I will be exalted among the heathen, I will be exalted in the earth" (Ps. 46:10). Our heavenly Father knows that we love this particular word. We love it because it exalts our heavenly Father to no limit. But our heavenly Father wants us to have a vivid comprehension of this precious scripture.

Why is it that we have to be still to know that God is God? Why can't we be moving and know that God is God? There is a reason why God said to be still. Still is defined; to place; set up; standing; immobile; without sound; quiet; silent; hush; soft or low in sound; not moving; stationary; calm; serene; motionless. If you receive this word (still) you will start to see God move in your life in manifestations and miracles. Every word of God is significant. It doesn't matter how small or large it is. Every word of God has been purified. " The words of the Lord *are* pure words; *as* silver tried in a furnace of earth, purified seven times" (Ps. 12:6). Therefore we must never overlook the word of God.

To be still is the key to knowing that God is truly God. When we define the word still the first definition was to place or set up; standing; immobile. This is truly remarkable. We tend to believe to be (still) is to lie down, on the contrary. It is essential that we stand or set up. You may sit down but you must be attentive. If we are lying down you can become to relaxed or perhaps fall asleep and you will never know that God is God. To be still means that you are immobile. You don't move your body physically and you do not speak. You are absolutely quiet. When you are in this state, then and only then, will you know that God is God.

God is not going to move in a miraculous way if you are hasty and monopolizing things on Earth. God will not come through or show up until we are still. When God shows up he wants everyone to know that it is him and not us. Therefore we have to be still. Then everyone around us will know that this power is certainly not the work of God's people, but indeed it is the power of God! If we are still then God gets all the glory and we get none. *Hallelujah!*

The Holy Spirit is saying it does not matter how many gifts he has given you, our heavenly Father must still receive the glory. If the Holy Spirit gives you a gift of healing, the person or persons that are healed must under-stand and believe that God did this and not the person God gave the gift to. The results should be the persons who are healed should always glorify God and thank Jesus for their deliverance and not us. Then we will know even though God has given us the manifestations of the gifts we were (still) enough for God to receive his glory.

Whenever we want God to move in a miraculous way, we always have to be still. Even if he is using us as instruments or if he just shows up. Regardless, we have to be yielded and still. This is why the prophet Zechariah declared, "Be silent, O all flesh, before the Lord: for he is raised up out of his holy habitation" (Zech. 2:13). If we want to see Holy Ghost power try being still for a time and witness God raising up out of his holy habitation. Then you will see the miracles you have read about in his holy word. God wants these miracles to take place today. Nothing has changed, "Jesus Christ the same yesterday, and today, and forever" (Heb. 13:8).

When we read the scriptures of how God's power is displayed in a miraculous way, you will always see immobility. Somehow our flesh becomes inactive. This is the wonderful uniqueness of being still. Moses knew this glorious secret, " And Moses said unto the people, Fear ye not, stand still, and see the salvation of the LORD, which he will show you today: for the Egyptians whom ye have seen today, ye shall see them again no more for ever" (Ex. 14:13). This was prior to crossing the Red Sea. The Israelites had fear that the Egyptians would kill them in the wilderness. But Moses said, fear not and stand still, stand still. It was imperative for the Israelites to stand still. This would be the only way that God would move supernaturally.

Moses continued to say " The Lord shall fight for you, and ye shall hold your peace" (Ex. 14:14). What Moses was saying is to hold your peace; be quiet; don't say a word; stand still; not sit, but stand as if you don't even exist; and get out of the way and watch God move. The Spirit of the Lord came through a still yielded vessel, which was Moses. And the Lord said unto Moses, "But lift thou up thy rod, and stretch out thy hand over the sea, and divide it: and the children of Israel shall go on dry *ground* through the midst of the sea" (Ex. 14:16). And God continued to say " And the Egyptians shall know that I *am* the Lord..." (Ex. 14:18).

Saints, this is what being still is all about. Everyone knowing that it is the Lord and not us. This divine purpose wasn't just for the Israelites, but also for our adversaries. After the victory of crossing over the Red Sea Moses and the children sang a song unto the Lord. This was one of the verses, "Fear and dread shall fall upon them; by the greatness of thine arm they shall be *as* still as a stone; till thy people pass over, O Lord, till the people pass over; *which* thou hast purchased " (Ex. 15:16). These were the inhabitants on the other side of the Red Sea. While the children were crossing over the Red Sea, the inhabitants were struck with fear and they were still as a stone. And they couldn't do anything but watch the Israelites cross over and possess the land that they had. God with his own arm made the adversary to be still as a stone until his children passed over. When God moves like this everyone must be still!

Jesus Christ knew about being still. When Jesus received the report that Lazarus was sick he did not go to minister to him immediately. John stated, "When he had heard therefore that he was sick, he abode two days still in the same place where he was" (John 11:6). Jesus stayed where he was still two days. He wasn't active throughout the community, but he was still. Lazarus died not long after this, and by Jesus being still God moved miraculously and Jesus raised Lazarus from the dead. Read John 11:1-46.

If we want to see the miracles that we read about in God's holy word, we must be still. Then, everyone will know that I am God, saidst the Lord. Beloved, know the power in this precious word. "But the Lord *is* in his holy temple: let all the earth keep silence before him" (Hab. 2:20). Amen.

Chapter Eight:
Overcome Evil with Good

"Be not overcome of evil, but overcome evil with good"(Rom. 12:21). How often do we hear this particular scripture? It rings in our ears every time our adversaries confront us. It echoes in our souls when we are tempted to repay evil for evil. To many saints, this scripture is difficult to do. James said, "But be ye doers of the word, and not hearers only, deceiving your own selves" (James 1:22). James proclaimed that we must do what the word tells us to do and not just hear it. In doing so there comes many blessings. Consequently, if we just listen or hear the word without applying or doing it the repercussions are grim. We will deceive ourselves. You will never know the bless benefits of God's word if you don't simply do it!

We will deceive ourselves because there are two phases in being blessed by God's word. You must first hear the word and secondly you must do it. When we come before our heavenly Father to hear his bless word, we become joyful and excited about what he has to say to us. Then we leave his presence and if we do not apply the word to our lives or do it, we are left feeling void or unaccomplished, not measuring up, or confused, often times accusing others for no victory in our lives. This is the deception that Saint James warns us about, by not doing what the word says to do.

Our heavenly Father does not want you to be deceived. It does not matter what word God has given you, it must be applied and you must do it in order for the scripture to be fulfilled. God knows this can be difficult for his people, but God has come to a point where he is saying "enough", enough darkness, enough defeat, enough bondage, enough captivity. The shackles are coming off! God no longer wants his people to be blinded or in darkness. Victory has prevailed, you must believe it!

Our heavenly Father wants you to overcome evil with good. The Holy Spirit has taught you that you must do what the word says opposed to just hearing it. How does one overcome evil with good? Paul proclaimed, "Be not overcome of evil, but overcome evil with good"(Rom. 12:21). Overcome is defined; to get the better of in competition, struggle; conquer; to master; prevail over; overpower or overwhelm; to be victorious; win. God does not want us to be conquered or to get the better of by evil, but to conquer or to get the better of evil with good. How glorious this will be when we master this scripture. This will be true victory!

We hear this scripture but we can deceive ourselves if we do not do it. Then we are left feeling that Romans 12:21 does not apply to our lives because we see no evidence of a blessing. You must do it order for the blessing to come. God's word does not always apply just for you. There is so much power in overcoming evil with good. If you hear and do what Romans 12:21 says, you can change lives and the course of history.

Romans 12:20 and the Proverbs declares, "If thine enemy be hungry, give him bread to eat; and if he be thirsty, give him water to drink: For thou shall heap coals of fire upon his head, and the Lord shall reward thee." (Prov. 25:21-22). This is overcoming evil with good. It is very difficult to give your enemy bread when he is hungry or water when he is thirsty. There is so much deliverance and liberty for your enemy in doing and not just hearing what this word says. When you do what God says, you will heap coals of fire upon your enemy's head. This will deliver your enemy from the bondage of hate that he has toward you. The coals of fire will actually burn or purge the sin out of your enemy's life. In doing so, one can be loose from the torment of hate toward you and others. And light days for him are near. Isaiah proclaimed he was undone because his lips were unclean and that he had seen the King, Lord of Host. Isaiah continued to say, "Then flew one of the seraphim unto me, having a live coal in his hand, *which* he had taken with the tongs from off the altar: And he laid *it* upon my mouth, and said, Lo, this hath touched thy lips; and thine iniquity is taken away; and thy sin purged." (Is. 6:6-7). Isaiah unclean lips were purged (cleansed) by the live coal that the seraphim laid upon his mouth. The coal was hot because the seraphim used the tongs to pick up the coal from the altar. This hot coal burned and took away Isaiah's iniquity. And he was cleansed from his sin. The coals of fire that you heap on your enemy's head will take away their sins. What the Holy Spirit is saying is that he will burn away the sin if you just trust God and hear his word and do it. We cannot think just of ourselves when God tells us to feed or to give drink to our enemies. There is a reason why God tells us to do this. In doing so God promise to reward you. You must believe it!

Stephen was a saint who wasn't just a hearer, but a doer of the word, even until his death. Stephen's enemies stoned him to death, read Acts 7: 54-60. Before Stephen fell asleep (die), he prayed a prayer, "And he kneeled down, and cried with a loud voice, Lord, lay not this sin to their charge. And when he had said this, he fell asleep" (Acts 7:60). Stephen overcame evil with good. What benefit did it do since Stephen died? Stephen changed the course of history with his prayer. Saul was among the adversaries that stoned Stephen. Saul consented unto Stephen's death and kept the raiment of the adversaries that slew Stephen. Read Acts 22:17-20. This was before Saul was converted. After Saul conversion, his name was changed to Paul. Beloved, if Stephen had not overcome evil with good, and prayed that prayer, Paul would not have been the apostle that he is today. Saul persecuted the church along with consenting to Stephen's death. Saul and the others were Stephen's enemies, but Stephen prayed a prayer and he asked God not to charge or let this sin be recorded against them. To let it be wiped away clean. Stephen heaped coals of fire on Saul and the other's heads by overcoming evil with good, and Saul was purged from his sins. And Jesus Christ chose Saul, who became Apostle Paul, to change the course of history. "But the Lord said unto him, Go thy way: for he is a chosen vessel unto me, to bear my name before the Gentiles, and Kings and the children of Israel:" (Acts 9:15). Hallelujah!

Jesus Christ is the epitome of overcoming evil with good. At Jesus crucifixion he prayed a similar prayer to God. "Then said Jesus, Father, forgive them; for they know not what they do..." (Luke 23:34). Father God, we pray that you will bless every soul that reads this letter. We pray, in the name of Jesus Christ, that you will do something new in each heart this day. God give your people a brand new start to be doers and not just hearers of your word, we pray God, we pray do this for your people! God let them be empowered by the Holy Ghost to overcome every evil with the goodness of you. God, take your word and do a miracle in every heart, and never let them see this blessed word from Jesus Christ the same again. Let this word transform their lives and do a work in them that only you can do. In the name of Jesus we pray. And Jesus said, "But I say unto you, Love your enemies, bless them that curse you, do good to them that hate you, and pray for them which despitefully use you, and persecute you;" (Matt. 5:44). Amen.

Chapter Nine:
The Blood of Jesus

❧

"For if the blood of bulls and of goats, and the ashes of a heifer sprinkling the unclean, sanctifieth to the purifying of the flesh: How much more shall the blood of Christ, who through the eternal Spirit offered himself without spot to God, purged your conscience from dead works to serve the living God?" (Heb. 9:13-14). This is the question that is proposed to the saints, how much more, how much more? When we think of the power of the *blood* it makes our whole being in awe. If the blood of animals can sanctify and purify your flesh, our heavenly Father is asking how much more will the *blood* of Jesus, through the Holy Spirit, will cleanse your conscience from dead works to serve the living God.

Dead works are works that are dead. They are no longer alive. They died with the old man. These works would have lead us to death, but because of the *blood* of Jesus Christ, they are purged (cleansed). Most Christians know it was the *blood* of Jesus that cleansed them from their sins. "In whom we have redemption through his blood, the forgiveness of sins, according to the riches of his grace;" (Eph. 1:7). We believe this and we hold this promise so close to our hearts. We count and rely on the *blood* of Jesus. If it was not for Jesus *blood*, the wrath would remain on us. "But God commendeth his love toward us, in that while we were yet sinners, Christ died for us. Much more then, being now justified by his blood, we shall be saved from wrath through him" (Rom. 5:8-9). We are ever so grateful for the precious blood of Jesus Christ.

But many saints do not realize the power and the extent of the *blood* of Jesus. We tend to know about the cleansing for our sins, but what about purging our conscience. As we stated earlier, the dead works no longer exist. They are inoperative, because they are dead. These works were active when we were in a sinful state, but if you confess your sins to God, he will cleanse you from these works. "If we confess our sins, he is faithful and just to forgive us our sins, and to cleanse us from all unrighteousness" (I John 1:9). But somehow some of the saints are still thinking about the dead works. Although the dead works are blotted out because of Jesus *blood,* our conscience is retaining these works, therefore the sin remains in our minds and in our hearts. And we are unable to serve the living God. If our works were not dead, we could not serve the living God. How could we if in our conscience we are reminded of the works that are dead. These dead works can be removed from your conscience. Some of you have tried to remove them by prayer or singing spiritual songs to block it out, or pretending they don't exist. There is only one things that can purge your conscience from the dead works and that is the *blood* of Jesus.

Conscience is defined having a feeling or knowledge of oneself as a thinking being; the part of a person mental activity of which he is fully aware at any time. This is the problem, at any given time the dead works can come back to your mind and to your hearts because the *blood* is not applied to your conscience. Although our conscience will do this from time to time this doesn't mean that there isn't any deliverance. Our heavenly Father wants you to know that the power of the *blood* of Jesus is not just for our sins, but it is also for our conscience. If we do not take advantage of the *blood* of Jesus, then the enemy will creep in having you to think about the dead works. This cannot happen because, our primary beings is to serve the living God. God doesn't want us serving him constantly thinking and repenting over and over about dead works. "THEREFORE   leaving the principles of the doctrine of Christ, let us go on unto perfection; not laying down the foundation of repentance from dead works, and of faith toward God" (Heb. 6:1). When we serve God we must serve him in all holiness and pureness, whether it is with our flesh or conscience. "Who shall ascend into the hill of the Lord? Or who shall stand in his holy place? He that hath clean hands, and a pure heart; who hath not lifted up his soul unto vanity nor sworn deceitfully" (Ps. 24:3-4).

The question that was proposed was, how much more shall the *blood* of Christ purge your conscience from dead works to serve the living God? The answer is a lot more. If Jesus *blood* can cleanse your sins, surely his *blood* can purge (cleanse) your conscience. YOU MUST BELIEVE IT! We know about the power of the *blood* that takes our sins away. We must know about the power of the *blood* that can purge or conscience from dead works also. As we plead the *blood* over our sins, we must also plead the *blood* over our conscience. You can do this today start to practice it. Whenever your past sins or dead works evoke, plead the *blood* over your conscience. You have to start by practicing and applying it. Paul made it an effort to keep his conscience in check. "And herein do I exercise myself, to have always a conscience void of offense toward God and *toward* men" (Acts 24:16). Paul made it a practice to exercise himself of not offending God or any of God's people. Therefore, his conscience was clear of offenses and of dead works. This would enable Paul to serve the living God.

In the name of Jesus, we pray God that every soul that reads this letter, that their conscience will be purged with the *blood* of Jesus. We rebuke every unclean and unholy thoughts that are no longer active, in the name of Jesus. We rebuke every dead work in your people's conscience, in the name of Jesus. We plead the *blood* over your people and their descendant's conscience, in the name of Jesus. Do a knew thing in every heart and mind this day. O God purge us with your son's *blood*. We lift up holy hands and receive the cleansing over our conscience. We thank you for delivering us from all of our dead works. We thank you for the power of the *blood* and how we are now able to serve you freely without restrictions. We thank you that we are able to bless and to serve you the living God. "Let us draw near with a true heart and full assurance of faith, having our hearts sprinkled from an evil conscience and our bodies washed with pure water. Let us hold fast the profession of *our* faith without wavering; (for he is faithful that promise;) And let us consider one another to provoke unto love and to good works:" (Heb. 10:22-24). Amen.

Chapter Ten:
"Hide Me In Your Heart..."

"Thy word have I hid in my heart, that I might not sin against thee" (Ps. 119:11). How precious is this scripture. We constantly quote this word, believing if we hide God's word in our hearts we will not sin against him. This is very profound and our heavenly Father takes us literally when we quote it. When we tell God that we will take his word and hide it in our hearts, God is watching us to see if we are committed to his word. God's word is available to us and at many times we apply it to our lives. But to hide it in our hearts is another benefit of God's word. What would we benefit from hiding God's word in our hearts? Primarily we would not sin against God, this is a promise saints, if you hide God's word in your hearts, the word says you will not sin against him. You must believe it!

Hiding is very powerful in itself. Hiding has always been one of the revelations in how our heavenly Father relates and communicates with his children. But in this area it is not God who is hiding, it is God's people taking this awesome technique of the word and applying it to their lives. This technique is hiding. Hide is defined to put or keep out of sight; to conceal from the knowledge of others, keep secret, to keep from being seen by covering up. This is one of the secrets of not sinning. The Psalms declares, "The law of his God *is* in his heart; none of his steps shall slide" (Ps. 37:31). The law is the word, and if the word is in your heart, or hidden, you are guaranteed not to slide (sin).

Why does the word have to be hidden or concealed in order for us not to sin? Why can't we just know and do what the word says and reap the benefits thereof? Jesus mother, Mary, knew exactly why we have to hide the word. In Luke, the angel of the Lord told the shepherds that a Savior was born which was Christ the Lord. And the angel told the shepherds where to find baby

Jesus, wrapped in swaddling clothes, lying in a manger with Mary and Joseph at his side. The shepherds told everyone abroad what was told to them concerning this baby Jesus. The scriptures continue to say " But Mary kept all these things, and pondered *them* in her heart" (St. Luke 2:19). Mary pondered or meditated in her heart, the shepherds went and told everyone abroad. Mary knew not to do this, instead she meditated, or thought deeply in her heart, concerning this matter. Mary wouldn't tell anyone about Jesus, (which is the word). Although Mary was fully aware that baby Jesus was the Savior, she never revealed it.

The angel, Gabriel, was sent from God and told Mary the destiny of Jesus. Read Luke 1:26-38. It was not the season for it to be revealed, so Mary hid the word in her heart. Why? The enemy would have stolen the word if she did not hide it. But the word was already out, and Herod the king heard it and wanted to destroy baby Jesus. Read Mathew 2:13. " The thief commeth not, but for to steal, and to kill, and to destroy..." (John 10:10). Mary knew she had to hide the word, which was Jesus, in her heart that she might not sin against God. If she didn't conceal this matter, God's plan would have been revealed and the enemy would have had this information. And Mary would have been out of the will of God. "For it is God which worketh in you both to will and to do of *his* good pleasure" (Phil. 2:13).

Although the enemy, Herod, knew part of the plan, he did not know it all. Saints we have to take heed and hide the word of God in our hearts also. There are times when God gives us a word and we share it by witnessing, teaching and preaching, this is not the circumstance. What the Holy Spirit is saying is that when God gives you a word and you do not hide it, the thief will come and try to steal it. And when the word is stolen you do not have anything to live on. " Jesus said 'Verily, verily I say unto you, If a man keep my saying he shall never see death'" (John 8:51). Keeping Jesus saying is keeping the word, you will not sin and you will also escape death. This speaks of the eternal death after the return of Jesus Christ.

Beloved, when God gives you a prophetic word, you have to be careful whom you share it with. If you share it with the enemy, he will steal the word that God has given you. This is why a lot of the prophecies have not come to pass yet, because we have revealed it to the wrong source. Prophecies will come to pass if it is from our heavenly Father, rests assure, but the enemy can slow it down by getting us out of the will of God. It is not God's will for all prophecies, which is the word of God, to be revealed to everyone, nor are we to reveal or share everything God has given us to our adversaries. Hezekiah fell into this trap by revealing his treasures and blessings to his adversaries. The prophet Isaiah gave Hezekiah a strong warning of the repercussions. Read II Kings 20:14-19. Saints, you must not reveal everything God has given you and done for you. You will know this by the Spirit. We have to have wisdom like Mary and hide the word in our hearts. There will be occasions when we will reveal prophecies, revelations and visions, but we must be lead by the Holy Spirit.

"Jesus said unto him, Thou shalt love the Lord thy God with all thy heart, and with all thy soul, and with all thy mind. This is the first and great commandment. And the second *is* like unto it, Thou shalt love thy neighbour as thyself. On these two commandments hang all the law and the prophets" (Matt. 22:37-40). This was Jesus response to a deceitful question. The question was which commandment was the greatest in the law? Jesus said unto him, "Thou shalt love the Lord thy God with all thy heart, and with all thy soul, and with all thy mind" (Matt 22:37). This was Jesus phenomenal response, that we are to love God with all of our hearts. The heart is the first issue that Jesus deals with. The mind and the soul come afterward but just as significant. God always deals with our hearts first. This is all he sees, "...for the *Lord seeth* not as man seeth; for man looketh on the outward appearance, but the Lord looketh on the heart" (I Sam. 16:7). Jesus knew that our hearts have to be right before God. If we love God with all of our heart and not half or a portion then God could truly use us for his glory. God wants us to love him with our whole hearts, he will not settle for less. You must believe it! How do we do this, by praying a prayer of David. "Hide thy face from my sins and blot out all my iniquities. Create in me a clean heart, O God; and renew a right spirit within me" (Ps. 51:9-10). Then we will be able to hide God's word in our hearts.

Jesus said "For out of the heart proceed evil thoughts, murderers, adulteries, fornications, thefts, false witness, blasphemies:" (Matt. 15:19). If you hide the word in your heart these sins cannot come to pass. This is why the Psalms proclaims if we hide the word in our hearts we will not sin against God. Sin comes out of the heart, and if the word is hidden in your heart, when the sin creeps in, the word, which is Jesus, is stronger every time. Sin can never stay where there is the word because Jesus is bigger and stronger and tougher and greater than anything or anyone. "Ye are of God, little children, and have overcome them: because greater is he that is in you, than he that is in the world" (I John 4:4). Amen.

Chapter Eleven:
Don't Faint

"And let us not be weary in well doing: for in due season we shall reap, if we faint not" (Gal. 6:9). This scripture hits the deep core of our being. Many saints thrive on this word, yet this is the word of God but to many saints weeping prevails when they hear or read this word from God. Our heavenly Father gave us this word through the apostle Paul. This is a strong but promising word from God. It is a strong word because God is telling us not to be weary in well doing. Weary is defined; growing tired or giving up, exhausted, tedious.

This word hits the heart of every saint because most saints are doing well. Doing well would be considered preaching and teaching the word of God., feeding the hungry, laying hands on the sick, ministering to the incarcerated, praying for Jerusalem, loving and praying for your enemies praying world wide salvation. And the list is endless of the saint's well doings. The well doings are remembered by God. Our heavenly Father has not forgotten any of your well doings. It can seem as though God has forgotten you because the enemy would have you to believe this, so you can faint or loose heart. If you faint or loose heart then you will not be able to receive your harvest. Don't faint!

King David was confronted with a dilemma. The Amalekites had invaded Ziklag and destroyed it with fire. And they took the women and their sons and daughters into captivity. David took this to heart because he loved God's people, and two of them were his wives. David and the people wept until they had no power left to weep. But King David had to make a decision would he faint, lose heart, or be courageous? I Samuel 30:6 says "...but David encouraged himself in the Lord his God". David didn't faint or lose heart, read 1Sam. 30:1-6. Sometimes you have to encourage yourself, especially when the enemy has stolen from you or you are being harassed by him. Nevertheless, do not faint!

Job testifies of a perfect scenario of being harassed by the enemy and never fainting. Job was attacked and harassed by his miserable friends he called them. They constantly insulted him. Job knew all of the things he had done that would be considered well doing. Nevertheless when his friends didn't see the harvest any longer they decided to attack his mind with insults to injury. This took a toll on Job and he began to lose heart. Job also testified about how being weary doesn't just affect you spiritually, but physically also. "But now he hath made me weary: thou hast made desolate all my company. And thou hast filled me with wrinkles, *which* is a witness *against me:* and my leanness rising up in me beareth witness to my face" (Job 16: 7-8). Here Job is testifying how being weary can actually cause you to prematurely age. The wrinkles on your face will actually witness or tell on you. And also a consuming amount of weight loss will also witness or tell on you. You won't be able to hide it. The saints and all the people of God will take notice. Beloved, if being weary can age your face, what does it do to your heart? your heart is not designed to take this type of stress. If your heart is prematurely aging, so will your life. Do not be weary in well doing., You must believe it!

Paul continues to say "...for in due season we shall reap if we faint not" (Gal. 6:9). If you sow you shall reap and Apostle Paul talks about what type of reaping you will receive based on the type of sowing you are doing. Read Gal. 6:8. If you are doing well in due season you will reap a wonderful harvest if you don't faint. The secret is due season. There is a season that is due to you and no other. Every man has his own season. When you see a brother or a sister harvest come forth rejoice, because yours is on the way. Their season is not your season. There is a set time that is due only for you and no other man. You must believe it! Only our heavenly Father knows this time. Your season is right around the corner, but if you faint or lose heart you will never receive that gigantic harvest of yours. You won't receive it spiritually, physically, financially and most of all everlasting (salvation). Paul declares "... but he that soweth to the Spirit shall of the Spirit reap life everlasting" (Gal. 6:8). Hallelujah!

Beloved, do not lose heart, encourage yourself the way David did and be like that tree he talked about. "And he shall be like a tree planted by the rivers of water, that bringeth forth his fruit in his season..." (Ps. 1:3). Here this man is blessed whom David is speaking of. And he compares him to this incredible tree. Take notice that this tree or man shall bringeth forth his fruit in his season, in his season, in his season! Saints, every man has a due season, every man has his own season. You must believe it! If you do become weary look to the one who has paid the price and has completed and finished everything just for you. Consider what he has done for you and meditate on it. God promises you, if you do this you will no longer be weary or faint.

"Looking unto Jesus the author and finisher of *our* faith; who for the joy that was set before him endured across, despising the shame, and is set down at the right hand of the throne of God. For consider him that endured such contradiction of sinners against himself, lest ye be wearied and faint in your minds" (Heb. 12:2-3). Amen.

Chapter Twelve:
The Cross

As born again believers when we think about our Lord and Savior Jesus Christ, we tend to think about salvation or his ressurection. It is seldom that we think of the cross. Perhaps it is because Jesus blessed assurance that his word was finished on the cross years ago. "When Jesus therefore had recieved the vinegar he said, It is finished: and he bowed his head, and gave up the ghost" (John 19:30). Yes, this is true, Jesus Christ work is finished. Jesus commandment was to finish and complete our heavenly Father's will. "Jesus saith unto them, My meat is to do the will of him that sent me, and to finish his work" (John 4:34). Jesus Christ work was our heavenly Father's will, and Jesus said , " For I came down from heaven, not to do my own will, but the will of him that sent me. And this is the Father's will which hath sent me, that of all which he hath given me I should lose nothing, but should raise it up again at the last day. And this is the will of him that sent me, that everyone which seeth the Son, and beleiveth on him, may have everlasting life: and I will raise him up at the last day" (John 6:38-40).

Jesus did finish this on the cross, but it doesn't stop here for the believers. A lot of saints believe that because Jesus Christ work is done on the cross and there remains nothing for them to do. This assumption is the furthest from the truth. Paul declared, "For the preaching of the cross is to them that perish foolishness; but unto us which are saved it is the power of God "(I Cor. 1:18). The cross is very powerful in itself. It is so powerful Decjust the preaching about it is the reason why we are saved. Hallelujuah! To the world it is foolish, unfortunately this is tragic, but to us it is eternal life. We must not forget about the cross saints. Many of us have forgotten about it because Jesus is in heaven with our heavenly Father and he is no longer on the cross. Your salvation has been affected for years, therefore, you asking yourselves, why reminence on the past? I beseech you, never forget what Jesus has done for you on the cross. There is still power on the cross! There are so many people of God who are not saved, we as believers must believe in the power of the cross for their salvation also. Jesus isn't on the cross any longer, but this does not mean the cross without him is powerless. Always remember it was the preaching of the cross that saved you.

Many of God's people are afraid that if they think of the cross they will remember their past sins. This is virtually impossible, by being born again those sins were nailed to the cross. "And you, being dead in your sins and the uncircumcision of your flesh, have hath quickened together with him, having forgiven you all trespasses; Blotting out the handwriting of ordinances that was against us, which was contrary to us and took it out of the way, nailing it to his cross (Col. 2:13-14). You must believe it! It is a wonderful thing to remember the cross and always boast about it, Paul certainly did, "But God forbid that I should glory save in the cross of our Lord Jesus Christ, by whom the world is crucified unto me, and I unto the world" (Gal. 6:14).

Jesus work is finished saints, but ours isn't. Our salvation is solid. There is no work to do here, Jesus paid it all. Once you become saved there is a glorious promise that follows, this is the sealing of the Holy Spirit. Every believer will have this promise, "In whom ye also *trusted* after that ye heard the word of truth, the gospel of your salvation: in whom also after that ye believed, ye were sealed with that holy Spirit of promise" (Eph. 1:13). What the Holy Spirit is saying is once you have heard the gospel, the preaching of the cross, then you believe. Then comes the glorious promise of the sealing of the Holy Spirit. This is the promise that Jesus told us about. "If you love me, keep my commandments. And I will pray the Father, and he shall give you another Comforter, that he may abide with you forever; *Even* the Spirit of truth; whom the world cannot recieve, because it seeth him not, neither knoweth him: but ye know him; for he dwelleth with you, and shall be in you" (John 14:14-17). Once you are sealed with this glorious promise then you are able and equipt to preach or witness about the power of the cross.

There is much to do and say about the cross. The enemy would have you to believe that because Jesus Christ isn't on the cross, the cross is ineffective. Do not believe it, just think of everything that Jesus has done for you on the cross. Jesus was a sacrifice in exchange for our eternal life on the cross. His blood was atonement for our sins on the cross. He was wounded for our transgressions on the cross. The chastisement of our peace was upon him on the cross. And with his stripes we were healed on the cross. Peter declared, "Who his own self bare our sins in his own body on the tree, that we, being dead to sins should live unto righteousness: by whose stripes ye were healed" (I. Pet. 2:24). This tree Peter talks about here is the cross. Peter makes it very clear that you and I were healed a long time ago and can still claim that same healing today that was on the cross years ago. Although Jesus isn't on the cross, the power of it is still effective even today.

It is the cross saints. Saints, never forget the cross! We have to think of the cross often because our healing was originally on the cross. Although God is a healer he sent his son to finish his work on the cross. Jesus may not be on the cross any longer but the power of the cross will always and forever exist until Jesus returns, hallelujah!

Father, we pray that you will bless your people and strengthen and encourage them like never before. Never let them forget what Jesus Christ has done for them on the cross. We pray that they will always see the power of the cross and keep it near to their heart. Father, do something supernatural and make a transformation, give them a sign this day of the power of the cross. Touch your people now, we pray, just one touch from Jesus, just one. Thank you Lord, we give you the praise and glory for this and in everything in Jesus name we pray. "For

it pleased *the Father* that in him should all fullness dwell; And, having made peace through the blood of his cross, by him to reconcile all things unto himself; by him, I *say*, whether *they be* things in earth, or things in heaven"(Col. 1:19-20). Amen.

Chapter Thirteen: "Be Ye Holy, For I Am Holy"

This is the beginning of a new year saints. We all are very excited about how God is speaking to our hearts. This will be a year like no other, great expectations and a move of God is near. God's expectations are far and greater than we could ever expect. The prophet Micah declares that there are three requirements of the Lord "...and what doth the Lord require of thee, but to do justly, and to love mercy, and to walk humbly with thy God?" (Micah 6:8). Yes saints, to walk humbly with God could be a major task for some of God's people. God is a spirit and he is holy. In order for us to walk humbly with God we have to be holy like God, there is no other way.

The Holy Spirit is about to make a great move on the men and women of God. God has already prepared some of your hearts in the year two-thousand and three. The year of two-thousand and four will be like no other. God wants to strengthen and encourage the prophets and his people to prepare you for what is coming. There will be a move of God so rapid in this new year, if you're not prepared for it you will be lost. But those of you who are prepared and ready will be very excited about what God is about to do. The voice that crieth out is wisdom, he cries out a call to holiness, a call to holiness, a call to holiness! God wants his prophets to be holy. Many prophets are called saved and the holiness that they believe and live is in private. God wants this to stop, he wants you to come out and live a life of holiness.

Holiness is the only way we can walk humbly with God and be like him. "For I *am* the Lord your God: ye shall therefore sanctify yourselves, and ye shall be holy; for I *am* holy" (Lev. 11:44). This is not just for the old times saints. Peter also declared, " But as he which hath called you is holy, so be ye holy in all manner of conversation; Because it is written, BE YE HOLY; FOR

I AM HOLY" (I Pet. 1:15-16). This is a plea to every woman and man of God. The Lord is winding things up quickly. We have been commanded to preach and teach the word of God, now we must live it and set an example for God's people. They are watching us and God does not want to hear the excuse that the reason why his people wont sanctify themselves to live holy is because the priest are not holy. This can not be, priest are always holy. It was only the priest who could go into the inner courts, the holy of the holiness. If the priests are not holy, than God's people will not be holy. Our heavenly Father is not talking about salvation, but a call to holiness. If the priest are holy men and women of God, the people will be holy too.

Paul declared that when Jesus returns for the church it should be holy. And if we are holy this would mean a separation from the world. Then are we ever ready for the return of our Lord and Savior Jesus Christ. Always remember, when Jesus returns for his church, it must be holy. Paul declared, "That he might present it to himself a glorious church, not having spot, or wrinkle, or any such thing, but it should be holy and without blemish" (Eph. 5:27). Yes, a call to holiness, there is no other way, you must believe it! Are you willing to take that next step of consecrating yourself to God. Some of you are and God will be preparing you for this in the year two- thousand and four. Many of you have been asking for God to reveal his glory to you, now it is time, but you must be holy. Are you ready?

This move of God will display his power and glory only on the women and men of God who are holy. Holiness doesn't come by a denomination, but by a consecration unto God from the world, through Jesus Christ, by the Holy Ghost. It also does not come by being obedient to your call by teaching or preaching, but by living the word out. To many prophets the Holy Spirit has already communed with you in night visitations or in visions and dreams. You are the ones he is preparing for this move but God wants to reveal his glory to all his prophets. You must go after him like never before in desperation. God winked at how we were living, now God's face is about to shine forth. Get ready for the glory of God, it will manifest like never before. We will see miracles like the old times and some of us will experience his glory the way Moses did.

God spoke these words to Moses prior to the ten commandments, "Now therefore, if ye will obey my voice indeed, and keep my covenant, then ye shall be a peculiar treasure unto me above all people: for all the earth *is* mine: And ye shall be unto me a kingdom of priests, and a holy nation. These are the words which thou shalt speak unto the children of Israel" (Ex. 19: 5-6). God said Israel shall be a peculiar treasure, which is a special people and that they shall be a kingdom of priest and a holy nation. If we would live a holy life, and separate ourselves from the world, there would be nothing that God could not do through us. Just imagine we being holy just like God, how glorious this would be, everything would change. Then and only then will God's nation be holy. This is a glorious promise from God for all of his saints. Every saint can be holy, every saint will be holy and a priest through our Lord and Savior Jesus Christ. "But ye are a chosen generation, a royal priesthood, a holy nation, a peculiar people; that ye should show forth the praises of him who hath called you out of darkness into his marvelous light" (I Pet. 2:9).

Wonderful Jesus, we thank you that we will be become a holy nation because of you. Thank you for making us holy priests. We will always show forth our praises to you because we love you and we are so grateful for what you have done for us and what you are going to do. We know, dear Jesus, that we could never be holy without you. Father God we come to you through Jesus Christ praying that you will touch every woman and man of God right now. Meet every woman and man of God that makes a decision that they will consecrate themselves holy to you in the year two-thousand and four. We know that this is not just for ourselves, but also for the people of God. Use them Lord like never before, thank you Jesus. Father, let two-thousand and four be a year like they have never experienced. Let the hunger and the cry that your prophets have been having for you be met. Sanctify, consecrate each one with your abiding presence. Let your anointing flow from the crowns of their heads to the soles of their feet. Reveal your glory to them, O God we pray, in these last days before our master returns for his holy church, that we will keep your commandment, that is to be holy, holy, holy. There is no other way. Bless your prophet's descendants and their descendant's descendants. Touch them now through your mighty power. Let them feel your presence, your glory, as they read this letter. Prepare them for the year of two- thousand and four by consecrating them holy. Wonderful Jesus a cry for holiness to every man and woman of God. Jesus, we pray strength to strength and your grace to every prophet and let the communion of the Holy Spirit and the love of God be with every prophet. Father we thank you ever so much, in Jesus name we pray. Amen.

Chapter Fourteen:
A Living Sacrifice

"I BESEECH, you therefore, brethren, by the mercies of God, that you present your bodies a living sacrifice, holy, acceptable unto God, *which is* your reasonable service. And be not conformed into this world: but be ye transformed by the renewing of your mind, that ye may be prove what is that good, and acceptable, and perfect, will of God" (Rom. 12:1-2). What a powerful word from God this is! We often quote these two scriptures without realizing the dept of it. If we realize the dedication and sacrifice these scripture require, would we be eager to quote them as often as we do? Apostle Paul is making a plea here to the church. He said, I beseech you which is defined; to sought, to entreat, implore or beg. Paul is earnestly begging the saints to present their bodies to God. This dynamic word from our heavenly Father stands today, nothing has changed. "Jesus Christ the same yesterday, and today, and forever" (Heb. 13:8). God is still looking for some living sacrifices, are you willing to make a presentation unto him with your bodies?

In last month's letter to the church, the Holy Spirit challenged those of you who wanted to make a commitment to God by a consecration to holiness. He told you that those of you who are willing to take the next step, that he would prepare you in this new year of two-thousand and four. He also told you that the glory of God will be most tangible to some of you. This preparation is not as easy as quoting a scripture. When God beseeches you to be a living sacrifice your whole life will change. He wants to change evil to good, lies to truth and darkness to light. The only way that God can do this is through a sacrifice. Yes, Jesus Christ is the ultimate sacrifice. He died and rose again never to die again for our sins. "So Christ was once offered to bear the sins of many; and unto them that look for him shall he appear the second time without sin unto salvation" (Heb. 9:28). God is looking for a living sacrifice, are you willing to be one?

Jesus died that we might have eternal life. A blood sacrifice was needed for the atonement for our sins. Jesus Christ shed his blood for this ultimate sacrifice. Jesus Christ will always be the epitome of sacrifices. This is not what our heavenly Father is talking about. God wants a living sacrifice, one that will not die for the cause but will live for it. David knew the type of sacrifice that God wanted from man, " For thou desirest not sacrifice; else would I give *it:* thou delightest not in burnt offering. The sacrifices of God *are* a broken spirit: a broken and a contrite heart, O God, thou will not despise" (Ps. 51:16-17). One must have a broken spirit and a contrite heart, which is to be humbled and crushed. This is a wonderful process, because this is where God dwells. "For thus saith the high and lofty One that inhabiteth eternity, whose name *is* Holy; I dwell in the high and holy *place,* with him also *that* is of a contrite and humble spirit, to revive the spirit of the humble, and to revive the heart of the contrite ones" (Is. 57:15). This is the type of sacrifice God is looking for. He will not despise this type.

When Paul said to present your bodies, he didn't mean the way Jesus presented his body on the cross. What Paul meant is for us to dedicate and present ourselves (our bodies) to God. You have to give your body to God as an offering or a presentation. You will literally be surrendering your will, your might. You will no longer exist. You will be broken-hearted and your spirit will be broken into a million pieces. The results will be that you will be humbled and yielded. Then God can use you and there will be nothing he can't do through you. A sacrifice is an offering in exchange for something else. This would be all so very spiritual. You must believe it.

Before you become a living sacrifice you must go through several stages. First you must be broken to get self and will out of the way. Secondly, you must present your bodies to God. This would be yielding in every sense of the word. Presenting oneself is normally done alone, no man will be able to see you, therefore, judgment would not occur during this process. But there will be a notable and visual change that will take place. When you make this decision God will have dealt with your spirit already. When you are ready he will call you for the presentation.

Moses prayed for the presence of God. He beseeched God to show him his glory. God's glory passed by Moses and Moses saw the back parts of God. Moses could not see his face. "And he said, thou canst not see my face: for there shall no man see me, and live" (Ex. 33:20). Moses experienced something supernatural, the awesome presence of God. All of God's goodness passed before him. Some of us will experience God's presence like Moses. Perhaps not the same way Moses did, but there will be some type of encounter with the presence of God. This would be for those of you who have been yearning to know God in a closer way, like Moses. But once you have entered into the presence of God there will be a price. God will not let you be in his presence like this without it costing you. The cost would be the presentation you make to God. Once God allows you to get this close to him, he will then tell you to present yourself to him. Almost immediately after God's presence passed by Moses, take notice of what God said to Moses "And be ready in the morning, and come up in the morning unto mount Sinai, and present thyself there to me in the top of the mount. And no man shall come up with thee, neither let any man be seen throughout all the mount; neither let the flocks nor herds feed before that mount" (Ex. 34:2-3).

This is the presentation Paul is talking about in Romans 12:1. This is normally after God has revealed himself to you in some supernatural way. It doesn't have to be like Moses, it could be a dream or a vision or even a trance. You will know it because it will be an encounter with God like never before. And when you present yourself to God you must go alone like Moses. And when you go, you have to leave everything behind you. Only you and God will know what that would be. This simply means God comes first and everything else is second. The next stage, God will not accept your presentation unless you are holy. Paul said that you are to present your bodies as a living sacrifice, holy and acceptable unto God. Then Paul carefully tells us not to be like the world but we should be transformed by renewing our minds. This way God's good, acceptable and perfect will would be accomplished.

Romans 12:1-2 is easily quoted, but do you really mean it? Are you willing to pay the price? If so, then Romans 12:3-21 will be much clearer to you now. In order for God's good and acceptable and perfect will to be done, you will have to live out Romans 12:3-21. Read the entire chapter of Romans 12. Verses 3-21 will be the requirement of a living sacrifice. You will not be able to live out Romans 12:1-2 unless verses 3-21 is fulfilled. This is what God calls **a living sacrifice!** "To whom coming, *as unto* a living stone, disallowed indeed of men, but chosen of God, *and* precious, Ye also, as lively stones, are built up a spiritual house, a holy priesthood, to offer up spiritual sacrifices, acceptable to God by Jesus Christ" (I Pet. 2:4-5). Amen.

Chapter Fifteen:
The Beauty of Repentance

"Bring forth therefore fruits meet for repentance" (Matt. 3:8). This is John the Baptist stating that when one repents they must have more than a change of mind, but a change of heart. You have to turn around and bring forth good fruits. This is the understanding you must have in order for God to forgive you of your sins. Repenting is much more than a change of mind, you literally have to show it by bringing forth your fruits. It is the goodness of God that turns man to repentance. "... not knowing that the goodness of God leadeth thee to repentance?" (Rom. 2:4). Your fruits have to be good in order for God to put repentance in your heart. You must never bring forth bad fruits but good ones in order for repentance to take place.

When we repent God forgives us. When God forgives us he doesn't just remember our sins any longer there comes a blessing with repentance. One tends to believe if they repent for their sins, there remains nothing else for them. Therefore, they will make an attempt not to sin again out of obedience but yet there is a void. This is where the enemy comes in and ask the saints what did you get out of this? He will then tell you absolutely nothing. No beloved, when we bring forth fruits meet for repentance, then comes forgiveness from God. Every time God forgives us he blesses us! Every time God forgives us he blesses us! Every time God forgives us he blesses us! That is what you get out of it! This is why King David declared, "BLESSED *is he whose* transgression *is* forgiven, *whose* sin *is* covered. Blessed *is* the man unto whom the Lord imputeth not iniquity, and in whose spirit *there is* no guile" (Ps, 32:1-2). Every time you repent, and God forgives you, he then blesses you. You must believe it! David makes it very clear if your sins are forgiven God is going to bless you. God cannot forgive you until there is repentance. This is why the enemy would tell the saints you don't need to repent and that repentance is only for sinners. This is not the truth. The enemy does not want you to repent because he knows with repentance comes forgiveness from God and an incredible blessing. Never listen to him, always hearken to the voice of the Lord.

There comes many blessings with repentance. David stated when our sins are covered we are blessed. No longer are our sins covered because the atonement of our sins is not with the blood of animals but the blood of Jesus Christ. Therefore, our sins are not covered any longer but blotted out. "Repent ye therefore, and be converted, that your sins may be blotted out, when the times of refreshing shall come from the presence of the Lord; And he shall send Jesus Christ, which before was preached unto you:" (Acts 3:19-20). Here Peter ministers to the people about repentance, and immediately he tells them in verse twenty that after repentance God will send Jesus Christ into their life (salvation). This is the ultimate blessing for repentance. We have all experienced this momentous blessing. Every soul that reads this letter and is saved had to repent in order for Jesus Christ to enter into their hearts. "For all have sinned, and come short of the glory of God;" (Rom. 3:23). The key word for the saints in this scripture is (have sinned). Our sins should always be passed tense, behind us. This is the difference between a sinner and a saint. A sinner's sins is always with him, but a saint's sins should always be behind him because of his repentance.

O repentance, how wonderful is that word. Our heavenly Father wants you to have a vivid understanding of this precious word. Repentance was created by God for us to live a life free of sin. Our heavenly Father wants you to see the beauty and truth behind repentance and the distortion and lies. The beauty of repentance is always a blessing. You must believe it!

In Psalm 32, David continues to minister about repentance and forgiveness. In the third verse, you will quickly see the distortion and lies that comes without repentance. David declares, "When I kept silence, my bones waxed old through my roaring all day long" (Ps. 32:3). What David is saying here is that when he was silent and did not confess his sins and repent to God, his bones grew old. His body began to fail him. This all came about because of the roaring all day long. Roaring is defined; to make or utter a deep hoarse sound as a lion, thunder voice and anger. When you have a penitent heart you will be filled with anger, resentment and bitterness. Your days will be filled with frustration and murmuring. Consequently, this will cause your health to suffer a great deal.

In verse four David continues to say, "For day and night thy hand was heavy upon me..." (Ps. 32:4). We always want to have God's hand upon us, but not like this. We don't want God's hand to be heavy. When something is heavy on you it feels like a force. This is an indication that when we are saved God's hand is upon his people. But it becomes heavy when we have a penitent heart. What is so marvelous about this is that God will keep his hand heavy on you day and night. The heaviness or conviction will not leave until you repent. This is how much God loves you. What a God we serve! Anything that is heavy you want it to be removed because of the pressure. This is the beauty of it, God will never remove his hand from his saints. No matter where you go or stray he will always keep you with his right hand. But in order for God's hand not to be heavy, we must do what David did in the very next verse, " I acknowledged my sin unto thee, and my iniquity have I not hid. I said, I will confess my transgressions unto the Lord; and thou forgavest the iniquity of my sin" (Ps. 32:5). This is it saints, we must acknowledge our sins to God. Then his hand will no longer be heavy but a hand full of pleasure. "Thou wilt show me the path of life: in thy presence *is* fullness of joy; at thy right hand *there* are pleasures forever more" (Ps. 16:11). Beloved, this is the beauty of repentance.

David also stated that repentance is for the saints as well as the lost. "For this shall everyone that is godly pray unto thee in a time when thou mayest be found: surely in the floods of great waters they shall not come nigh unto him" (Ps. 32:6). There you have it, everyone that is godly and saved should always pray this way when they repent and are forgiven. When we do pray and repent for our sins this is a sure way we can find God. Many times when we pray we can't find him. Beloved, if there is a need for repentance you will never find him until repentance has taken place. The blessing behind this is that David assures us that the floods of great waters will not be able to touch us. In other words, we will never be overcome by the enemy's worst attacks, and his fiery darts will never touch us! "If we confess our sins, he is faithful and just to forgive us *our* sins and to cleanse us from all unrighteousness" (I John 1:9). Always remember the beauty behind repentance, that once you repent God forgives you, then he will always bless you. You must believe it! "My little children, these things write I unto you, that ye sin not. And if any man sin, we have an advocate with the Father, Jesus Christ the righteous: And he is the propitiation for our sins: and not for ours only, but also for *the sins of* the whole world" (I John 2:1-2). Amen.

Chapter Sixteen:
Do Not Be the Only
One, But Be One!

〜

Grace peace from God the Father and from our Lord and Savior Jesus Christ.

Beloved, our heavenly Father has a powerful and tender word for the church in the year of 2005. The Lord loves his church and he can't wait to be in complete unity with the body of Christ. The body of Christ will not be completed until it has the head, which is Jesus Christ. Jesus can not wait to gather the church, which is the body. The Spirit of the Lord says that, "Jesus yearns for his body, which is the church".

There are many of us who feel incompleteness or a void, this emptiness would be the head of our body, which is Jesus Christ. "And he is the head of the body, the church: who is the beginning, the first born from the dead; that in all *things* he might have the pre-eminence" (Col. 1:18). Yes beloved, many of us yearn to be with our Lord Jesus Christ, as he yearns to be with us. Why the desperation, because the time is at hand! Have you heard, or do you know already that Jesus Christ is about to return for his body, the church.

Beloved, the Spirit of the Lord has spoken to me to tell you this powerful and prophetic word, "DO NOT BE THE ONLY ONE, BUT BE ONE! DO NOTBE THE ONLY ONE, BUT BE ONE! DO NOT BE THE ONLY ONE, BUT BE ONE!" What does our heavenly Father mean by this? Jesus Christ spoke a prophetic word in a payer to our heavenly Father, "That they all may be one; as thou, Father, *art* in me, and I in thee, that they also may be one in us: that the world may believe that thou hast sent me" (John 17:21). Jesus prayed this prayer just hours away from his crucifixion. He also uttered prophetic words. Jesus prophesied that the church would be one and every word that Jesus Christ spoke has and will come to pass. The prophetic word that Jesus spoke was that the church must be one. This prophetic word must come to pass before Jesus returns for his body, the church.

The Spirit of the Lord is saying, "DO NOT BE THE ONLY ONE, BUT BE ONE!" Why is he saying this? Many of us are scattered into our own ministries, says the Spirit of the Lord. We so easily forget that we, the body of Christ, have to fit tightly together, leaving no spaces in order to be one as Jesus prophesied. "From whom the whole body fitly joined together and compacted by that which every joint supplieth, according to the effectual working in the measure of every part, maketh increase of the body unto the edifying of itself in love" (Eph. 4:16). Beloved we must try harder to come together and not declare that our ministries are the only ministries for Jesus Christ

Our heavenly Father loves all of his sons and daughters. There is no need for insecurity in this area. The Spirit of the Lord says many of us are scattered and believe that our ministries are the only ministries for Jesus Christ. Jesus Christ will not return until this prophetic word has come to pass. We have to start helping each other and stop being envious and insecure of others. This is not a game, it is about the kingdom of God. It doesn't matter how much we are equipped and anointed, we all have to jointly fit together, and be compacted (compressed, firmed) in unity with others. If we don't, Jesus will not return until this prophecy is fulfilled. The Spirit of the Lord says "DO NOT BE THE ONLY ONE, BUT BE ONE! DO NOT BE THE ONLY ONE, BUT BE ONE! DO NOT BE THE ONLY ONE, BUT BE ONE!".

Rests assure that Jesus, the head, will return for his body, the church. In John 17:21, Jesus stated that he was one with the Father, and that our Father God is one with Jesus Christ. Then he continues to pray, " ... that they also may be one in us: that the world may believe that thou hast sent me" (John 17:21). You see, beloved, the world will never believe that Jesus came from God the Father if we are scattered with our ministries. We have to be tightly fitted together in order for the world to believe that we are one. Once the world sees how close and tightly fitted the church is, then they will most definitely believe that JESUS IS LORD!

No one is going to believe what one has to say if all the facts are not together. Any type of presentation or declaration has to have all the facts pointing to its initial point that one is proposing. If you lack anything, you can so easily lose your point. We do not want to do this with the body of Christ. If the world looks and sees the church scattered with our own different denominations and beliefs, how can they then believe that Jesus Christ was sent from God for them. What do they have to convince them of this, certainly not individual ministries proclaiming that their ministries are the only ones. The world will believe when they see the church supporting the church, not the church supporting their ministries and denominations. Do not forget the mission that we are on, winning lost souls for Jesus.

Jesus Christ did not come to set up the perfect church on Earth, he came to take back the perfect church to heaven with everyone and anyone who believes that he is the son of God. "For God so loved the world, that he gave his only begotten Son, that whosoever believeth in him should not perish, but have everlasting life. For God sent not his Son into the world to condemn the world; but that the world through him might be saved" (John 3:16-17). This is what it is all about, beloved. Those prophetic words that Jesus prayed will come to pass. He will not return for a church that is scattered and self- motivated. Let us be faithful and obedient and feed off of these prophetic words of our Lord and Savior Jesus Christ.

Father, we pray as a body fitly joined together, that we will not be scattered, but one supporting the entire body of Christ. We thank you for the prophetic utterance of Jesus Christ, your Son. Father we realize that every word that Jesus spoke must, and will, come to pass. So let us be faithful in contributing to our part for the kingdom of God. We will prayerfully and willingly support the entire body of Christ and diligently pray that there will be no scattering or spaces, and that we will be fitly joined together and compacted. Father we thank you that you see the body of Christ as one and we thank you for Jesus Christ, our Lord and Savior. We pray, Father, that we will honor the prophetic word that was spoken to the body of Christ. "DO NOT BE THE ONLY ONE, BUT BE ONE! DO NOT BE THE ONLY ONE, BUT BE ONE! DO NOT BE THE ONLY ONE, BUT BE ONE!" That the world might believe that Jesus Christ was sent from you. In Jesus name we pray. Amen.

Chapter Seventeen:
If It is Not a Miracle, God is Not In It

Grace, peace from God our Father and from the Lord Jesus Christ.

Our heavenly Father has a powerful word for the church in the month of April. Our heavenly Father wants us to know that it is time for the miracles to begin! After all, we serve a God of miracles. Our heavenly Father does not know how to do anything less than a miracle. Our blessed Father wants us to start treating and acknowledging him as a God of miracles.

When we come to him with our petitions we are to always come prepared to ask for a miracle. If we do not ask our heavenly Father for a miracle, or expect a miracle, we will not get one. You cannot go to a fish market and ask for eggs. The fisherman would say, "As much as I would like to serve you, and as much as I would like to appease you, I cannot because I only sell fish. I cannot give you eggs because I do not sell eggs". You can proceed to plea with the fisherman and his answer will always be "No. I certainly cannot give you what you are asking for".

This is how it is with the body of Christ. Some of us are continually asking our heavenly Father for eggs, and he only has fish (which are miracles). We are making out request to the Lord and we are not receiving them because we are not asking for miracles. We have to have a complete comprehension of the type of God we serve. The God that we serve is a God of miracles! Start asking for miracles, and you will start to see miracles.

The spirit of the Lord saith, "KNOW THIS, IF IT IS NOT A MIRACLE, GOD IS NOT IN IT! IF IT IS NOT A MIRACLE, GOD IS NOT IN IT! IF IT IS NOT A MIRACLE, GOD IS NOT IN IT!" This is very powerful and life changing word from our heavenly

Father. Everything that Jesus did was a miracle. Every situation in all of the gospels were changed the moment Jesus Christ arrived on the scene. How did it change? It changed with miracles, signs and wonders.

Jesus Christ very first miracle was in Cana, Galilee, where he turned water into wine. This, no doubt, got the attention of many including his disciples. This miracle, indeed, witnessed that he is the Son of God. "This beginning of miracles did Jesus in Cana of Galilee, and manifested forth his glory; and his disciples believed on him" (John 2:11).

When Jesus mother, Mary, said they have no wine, in other words, they ran out of wine. Jesus reply to his mother was shocking! Jesus made it very clear to his mother, Mary, that this had nothing to do with him. Jesus said that it was not his time to be revealed concerning good works. Read John 2:2-4. But Mary knew more. Mary's reply was not to Jesus, but to the servants. "... Whatsoever he saith unto you, do *it*" (John 2:5). Mary knew more. Although Jesus said, it was not his time, indeed it was his time. This was the beginning of the Son of God's manifestation by miracles. Jesus Christ was always known for his miracles. In every situation with Jesus there was a miracle.

The Spirit of the Lord saith there will be more of a supernatural power of God released in the last days we are living in. Many of God's prophets, servants and ministers have been prepared and trained by the Holy Spirit. There are men and women of God who are equipped to do good works (miracles) unto the Lord. Read II Timothy 3:17.

Apostle Paul prophesied, in II Timothy 3:1, that in the last days perilous times shall come. He names a host of different sins men will be involved in. Read II Timothy 3: 2-5. What is so overwhelming is that this group is claiming salvation. Paul stated this about this group of people, "having a form of godliness, but denying the power thereof: from such turn away". (II Tim 3:5). This particular group will have a form (a shape, figure, image, or outline, no real substance) truly lacking a relationship with the living God. They will appear to live in godliness. To live in godliness, one has to seek to live in harmony and in accordance to God's will. As great as it seems, this will all be a form, or an image with this particular group.

Our heavenly Father does not want the church to be deceived. You will know them by their fruits, Jesus Christ declared. Read Matthew 7:15-20. A good tree, which is a person who is saved, cannot bring forth evil fruit. Neither can a corrupt tree, a person who is not saved, bring forth good fruit. Paul makes it very clear, in II Timothy 3:5, that although they have a form of godliness,(image) you will still know them, as Jesus declared, by their fruits.

The way you will most definitely know this deceiving group who claim salvation is that they will deny the Holy Spirit. They will deny signs and wonders and they will deny miracles. Paul continued to say, "... but denying the power thereof" (II Tim. 3:5). Yes beloved, a lot of them are mum about this, so it would be difficult to know without exercising your discernment.

The power of God is the Holy Spirit. "And Jesus returned in the power of the Spirit into Galilee...." (Luke 4:14). Beloved, this group will literally deny the Holy Spirit, but will proclaim salvation. If one denies the Holy Spirit. they will also deny miracles. The Holy Spirit does miracles through us. Peter declared, "... God anointed Jesus of Nazareth with the Holy Ghost and with power..." (Acts 10:38).

Beloved, take heed, but do not fret, Paul prophesied that this would come in the last days. And we are living in the last days now, Hebrews 1:1-2. The God of the heavens and the earth has anointed many of you with Acts 10:38! Some of you do not realize it is time to turn water into wine. You may say, no, it is not my time, but God knows more. It is your time! Preaching and teaching is wonderful, but many will not believe until they see signs and wonders. Read John 4:43-54.

Everyone does not have believing faith. So let the miracles begin! Are you ready to turn water into wine? God is looking for those who truly believe in miracles and do not deny the power of God and will not doubt him for anything. Are you ready to turn water into wine? The Spirit of the Lord saith, "KNOW THIS, IF IT IS NOT A MIRACLE, GOD IS NOT IN IT! IF IT'S NOT A MIRACLE GOD IS NOT IN IT! IF IT'S NOT A MIRACLE GOD IS NOT IN IT!"

Beloved, take this time to reflect over your walk with Jesus. Reflect on the things you have done for Jesus. Was it a miracle? If it was not a miracle, God was not in it. Oh beloved, how God loves you. Take a deep, long breathe as you read this letter. Now exhale, God is in it. That is a miracle. This reflection will also help you to know if you are in the will of God, referring to his kingdom. Do not you see the miracles have already begun? Now God wants you to take another step of faith. Are you ready to turn water into wine?

You may say, "The gift of miracles does not operate in me, how could God ever use me to turn water into wine?" All I do is preach and teach the gospel. Yes, yes, yes, salvation is the greatest miracle in the world! You have already begun. No man can move another man's heart and change it from stone to flesh! No man can convict a man's heart to repent of sins. And no man can bring you to Jesus if our heavenly Father had not drawn him to his Son. It's all a miracle. It is not us, God uses us. Are you ready to turn water into wine? This is the season for miracles, saith the Spirit of the Lord.

The Spirit of the Lord saith, "Great shall every man be in his own gifts. Seek not another ministry, focus on your own and make full proof of your ministry. Seek my face, saith the Lord, and not men. The Spirit of the Lord saith IF IT IS NOT A MIRACLE, GOD IS NOT IN IT! IF IT IS NOT A MIRACLE, GOD IS NOT IN IT! IF IT IS NOT A MIRACLE, GOD IS NOT IN IT!"

"But ye shall receive power, after that the Holy Ghost is come upon you: and ye shall be witnesses unto me both in Jerusalem, and in Judea, and in Samaria, and unto the uttermost part of the earth" (Acts 1:8). Amen.

Chapter Eighteen:
You Have Not Resurrected Unless You Are Walking By Faith

⤳

Grace, peace from God our Father and from the Lord Jesus Christ.

"Know ye not, that so many of us were baptized into Jesus Christ were baptized into his death? Therefore we are buried with him by baptism into death: that like as Christ was raised up from the dead by the glorify of the Father, even so we also should walk in the newness of life. For if we had been planted together in the likeness of his death, we shall be also in the likeness of his resurrection" (Rom. 6:3-5)

YOU HAVE NOT RESURRECTED UNLESS YOU ARE WALKING BY FAITH, SAITH THE SPIRIT OF THE LORD; Otherwise you are still dead. Baptism symbolizes resurrection. You were immersed under the water, the old man, then you came up the new man, the newness of Christ, not your way, no works, remember, no law, but grace and righteousness. We have won this battle. " That as sin hath reigned unto death, even so might grace reign through righteousness. We have won this battle. "That as sin hath reined unto death, even so might grace reign through righteousness unto eternal life by Jesus Christ our Lord" (Rom. 5:21).

What does righteousness have to do with walking in the newness of Christ? "Neither yield ye your members as instruments of unrighteousness unto sin: but yield yourselves unto God, as those that are alive from the dead, and your members as instruments of righteousness unto God" (Rom. 6:13). When you were baptized, the old man died under the water. " I am crucified with Christ: nevertheless I live; yet not I , but Christ liveth in me: and the life which I now live in flesh I live by the faith of the Son of God, who loved me, and gave himself for me" (Gal. 2:20). Paul stated, I am crucified with Christ, spiritually dead with Christ, the anointed one.

When you have received Jesus as Lord of your life you die to self and receive Jesus as your Lord. Paul stated "…nevertheless I live; yet not I." Although you are dead spiritually, you are also alive. It is not you "but Christ liveth in me: and the life which I now live in the flesh, I live by faith." This here refers to the resurrection for the saints. When you came up out of the water, you have been baptized to death. This is what Paul referred to earlier. "Know ye not, that so many of us were baptized unto Jesus Christ were baptized into his death?" (Rom 6:3) When you came up out of the water, you must walk by faith, then you will be resurrected with Christ. Paul continues to say, "… of the Son of God who loved me and gave himself for me". BELOVED, YOU HAVE NOT RESURRECTED WITH CHRIST UNLESS YOU ARE WALKING BY FAITH, SAITH THE SPIRIT OF THE LORD.

Many of you have heard the term "spiritually dead." Some of the saints are still spiritually dead. You have been baptized in the water, baptized into Jesus, which is baptism into his death (Rom. 6:3), but you came up out of the water and went your way. Many of the saints feel they have no real substance in their Christian walk. This would be because you are walking by sight. You have not encountered the resurrection of power. In order to obtain or to have resurrection power, after your resurrection from the old man, you must walk by faith. This is why Paul said, "… And the life which I now live in the flesh I live by faith of the Son of God who loved me, and gave himself for me" (Gal. 2:20). This is the only way you will have the resurrection power of Jesus Christ. Water baptism is all about faith. "… the substance of things hoped for, the evidence of things not seen" (Heb. 11:1). We are hoping for real resurrection power. There is power and there is resurrection power. Both of these powers come from God the Father and he gave his power to his Son, our Lord Jesus Christ. "And Jesus came and spake unto them, saying, All power is given unto me in heaven and in earth" (Matt. 28:18). There is an earthly power and a heavenly power. This heavenly power is the resurrection power. This power comes to us when we walk by faith only.

We can not take water baptism lightly, it is very important in the Kingdom of God. Water baptism symbolizes death. In order for you to be dead to sin your natural bodies must die to sin, to the point that when sin comes it will not affect you. This comes only by obedience and belief. "Knowing this, that our old man is crucified with him, that the body of sin might be destroyed, that henceforth we should not serve sin. For he that is dead is freed from sin,. Now if we be dead with Christ, we believe that we shall also live with him: Knowing that Christ being raised from the dead dieth no more; death hath no more dominion over him. For in that he died, he died unto sin once: but in that he liveth, he liveth unto God. Likewise, reckon ye also yourselves to be dead indeed unto sin, but alive unto God through Jesus Christ our Lord. Let not sin therefore reign in your mortal body, that ye should obey it in the lust thereof" (Rom. 6:6-12).

This is it saints! Our Lord wants us freed from sin, freed from bondage. But you must be obedient to this powerful word. You have to "reckon" that you are dead. (Rom. 6:11) This is the key, "reckon". Reckon is defined as, to direct, to count, to figure up, to think, to suppose, to depend, to consider. This all comes by your faith. Reckon is to think and consider and believing you are dead to sin. This is the only way! This would be the power of faith activating in your life!

After your water baptism you are not to walk in the lust thereof. "For all that is in the world, the lust of the flesh and the lust of the eyes, and the pride of life, is not of the Father, but is of the world (I John 2:16). When you walk by faith, those things will not affect you any longer. It doesn't matter what you see, the lust of the eyes will not affect you any longer. "(For we walk by faith, not by sight:)" (II Cor. 5:7). Although sin may appear or jump out at you, if you walk by faith you will not see it. Peter tells us, "...abstain from fleshly lust, which war against the soul" (I Peter 2:11). Do you believe it? "Being then made free from sin, ye became the servants of righteousness" (Rom. 6:18). THE SPIRIT OF THE LORD SAITH, YOU HAVENT RESURRECTED UNLESS YOU ARE WALKING BY FAITH.

How does being free from sin by walking in righteousness relate to one walking in the newness of Christ and his resurrection? In order for one to be free from sin, he must first be dead to sin (Rom. 6:6). Then he is able to walk in righteousness. If one is to walk in the newness of Christ and his resurrection as the Spirit of the Lord said, then you have to walk by faith. When we are servants of righteousness through grace, you have to walk by faith. "Even the righteousness of God which is by faith of Jesus Christ unto all and upon all them that believe…" (Rom. 3:22). This is the beginning stage, believing. "For God so loved the world, that he gave his only begotten Son, that whosoever believeth in him should not perish, but have everlasting life" (John 3:16). This blessing will only come to you if you believeth in Jesus Christ. Not just believing he is the Son of God, not just believing he died for our sins, but believing in everything that he, Jesus, taught! Jesus taught and commanded water baptism. Jesus approached John the Baptist about baptizing him. John didn't want to do this. He thought that Jesus should be baptizing him. "And Jesus answering said unto him, Suffer it to be so now: for thus it becometh us to fulfill all righteousness. Then he suffered him" (Matt. 3:15). Here Jesus himself was baptized to fulfill all righteousness. Everything has to be fulfilled by Jesus or else it can't be. Jesus commanded the disciples that they must baptize every believer. "Go ye therefore, and teach all nations, baptizing them in the name of the Father, and of the Son, and of the Holy Ghost" (Matt 28:19).

THE SPIRIT OF THE LORD SAITH YOU HAVE NOT RESURRECTED UNLESS YOU ARE WALKING BY FAITH. This is it beloved, in order to be truly resurrected, dead to sin, you have to walk by faith. If you have been baptized you should have been resurrected with Jesus Christ. Many of you have experienced water baptism, but never resurrected. This has nothing to do with your salvation, but a struggle with sin. There's a spiritual death when we are baptized, but some of you haven't resurrected as of yet. You have to be walking completely by faith. This is what defeats sin. If you are walking by sight, the adversary will always tempt you by this. But he can not touch you if you are walking by faith. Why? Because our believing faith is how we overcome. "For whatsoever is born of God overcometh the world: and this is the victory that overcometh the world, even our faith" (I John 5:4).

Yes beloved, in order for you to walk in the newness of Christ, which is to be sin free and resurrected, you have to walk by faith, saith the Spirit of the Lord. Many of the saint are disappointed because they know they have no resurrection power. You know you have been struggling with sin and have been saved for years, why? You are not walking in faith once you came out of that water! It's all a spiritual journey from then on. You do not go by what you see. Why do we keep saying this? Because you have to understand if you can see it, you have not resurrected! Spiritually, you are dead still buried with no resurrection (life) and definitely no resurrecting power. "While we look at all the things which are seen, but at the things which are not seen" for the things which are seen are temporal; but the things which are not seen are eternal" (II Cor. 4:18).

Things that are not seen would be walking by faith. Paul yearned for this. This is not an overnight experience but a process and he encouraged us to do the same. Paul knew that he could not have this resurrection power, or to walk in the newness of Christ, unless he is completely dead to sin. This would be walking in faith after the water baptism experience. Paul knew it was a complete surrender that could take a lifetime with Jesus Christ or sometime. To walk completely by faith is a process, but will greatly fulfill your life in every way. "and be found in him, not having my own righteousness, which is of the law, but that which is through the faith of Christ, the righteousness which is of God by faith: That I may know him, and the power of his resurrection, and the fellowship of his sufferings, being made comfortable unto his death (Phil. 3: 9-10).

Here Paul yearns for the resurrection power the way we all do. Paul continues to say, "If by any means I might attain unto the resurrection of the dead. Not as though I had already attained, either were already perfect: But I follow after if that I may apprehend that for which also I am apprehended of Christ Jesus" (Phil. 3:11-12). Paul makes it clear that he has not attained (arrived) completely unto the resurrection of the dead, but he acknowledged that he apprehended (which means to take hold or to take custody; captive, understand). This is what he and we need to do. What is wisdom without understanding? Many of you are in this area. Oh! Precious Lord, how we yearn to know the power of Christ's resurrection. Paul continues to say, I might not be perfect, I may not be there yet, but one thing I do have is an apprehension an understanding of the resurrection power. Paul said by the apprehension (understanding) I might not walk completely by faith since my death.

He continued to say, but one thing I know, everything in my past, my old sins, my old life, my old nature, I will not remember it any longer. It may not be all buried when I got baptized based on my lack of faith, but I tell you this, I will not remember it any longer! Paul said he will never look back, but always be looking toward his future and leaving the past behind him. And what is your past? Your past is anything that is not your future. Paul said all these things are behind him. These things are behind, they are buried, and he is reaching forward to his future by walking in faith. "Brethren, I count not myself to have apprehended: but this one thing I do, forgetting those things which are behind and reaching forth unto those things which are before. I press toward the mark for the prize of the high calling of God in Christ Jesus. Let us therefore, as many as be perfect, be thus minded..." (Phil. 3:13-15). Let us all press toward this mark and never give up. Never!

Our heavenly Father wants us to have an apprehension (understanding) that you can not be resurrected unless you walk by faith. If you are walking by faith after your baptism, then you have resurrected. If you are not, it is only because you are walking by sight. This would cause us to lack many promises of our heavenly Father. And your Christian journey could be difficult. Let us all go and walk completely by faith so we will all have the resurrection power of Jesus Christ. Indeed it is a challenge for us all. Remember, this has nothing to do with our salvation, but it can make all the difference in capturing the resurrection power we all yearn for. THE SPIRIT OF THE LORD SAITH YOU HAVE NOT RESURRECTED UNLESS YOU ARE WALKING BY FAITH.

Father, let us all know and have the resurrecting powering of Jesus Christ, give us a complete understanding of this wonderful power, never let us walk by sight, but by faith only, we pray; bless every saint that has read this letter; anoint them new and afresh, give them your resurrection power in the name of Jesus Christ; I speak this by the anointing that's on my life, that this resurrecting power may come upon you and stay with you until the coming of our Lord and Savior Jesus Christ, and unto him be all the glory and the praise forevermore. In Jesus name, it is done.

THE SPIRIT OF THE LORD SAITH YOU HAVE NOT RESURRECTED UNLESS YOU ARE WALK ING BY FAITH. " And ye are complete in him which is the head of all principalities and power. In whom also ye are circumcised with the circumcision made without hands, in putting off the body of the sins of the flesh by the circumcision of Christ: Buried with him in baptism wherein also ye are risen with him through the faith of the operation of God who hath raised him from the dead" (Col. 2: 10-12).

Chapter Nineteen:
Sow! Sow! Sow!

Grace, peace to you, from God our Father and from the Lord Jesus Christ.

"And laid *them* down at the apostles' feet: and distribution was made unto every man according as he had need. And Joses, who by the apostles was surnamed Barnabas, (which is, being interpreted, The son of consolation,) a Levite, *and* of the country of Cyprus, Having land, sold *it*, and brought the money, and laid *it* at the apostles' feet (Acts 4:35-37).

Dear beloved, when you see someone that has your destiny locked up inside of them, all you can do is look at them, because you can't get it out. All you can do is stare and cry, stare and cry. We pray, oh Lord, how can we get what is ours. Your destiny is like precious china locked up in a china cabinet. You stare and stare at the beauty. Oh! if you could only touch it.

How can we unlock the china cabinet door? I don't have the key, I dare not break the glass or shatter it because I love the china cabinet. I don't want to harm it. Oh! Dear Jesus, tell us how to unlock the china cabinet. Then I said "Oh, I know Master, you are the key. Please give me the key to my destiny." Then our Lord Jesus said, "No, I'm not the key, I am the door to the china cabinet." Precious Lord, how do I get my destiny that is locked up in the china cabinet? How do I get the key to unlock this door?

Then the Lord said, key means secret, wisdom. The Lord also said, "If any of you lack wisdom, let him ask of God, that giveth to all *men* liberally, and upbraideth not; and it shall be given him. But let him ask in faith, nothing wavering..." (James 1:5-6). The Lord also said "A double-minded man *is* unstable in all his ways (James 1:8). "Let this mind be in you, which was also in Christ Jesus" (Phil. 2:5). Beloved, do not have two minds, your mind and Christ mind are two minds. This beloved, is a double-mind, your mind and my mind, saith the Lord. Most of my people think this is well. No my little children, keep this mind in Christ, have the mind of Christ. You can no longer have your mind. "...THOU SHALT LOVE THE LORD THY GOD WITH ALL THY HEART, AND WITH ALL THY SOUL, AND WITH ALL THY MIND" (Matt. 22:37). No more your mind beloved.

Your mind mixed with my mind is a double- mind. Deny yourself and take up the cross, then you will have one mind. "...if any *man* will come after me, let him deny himself, and take up his cross, and follow me" (Matt 16:24). My mind, the mind of Christ, not your mind, no double-mind. And when you have my mind then you will have the wisdom and know the secret of the mind of Christ. Beloved, you now have the key, now put the key in the lock and I will open the door. And I said, "Oh Jesus, how beautiful this China is" and the Lord said, "DESTINY EMBRACES YOU".

This is the wisdom of the Lord, truly "... It is more blessed to give than to receive" (Acts 20:35). Barnabas knew this. He had the key (wisdom, secret) to his china door being open. Barnabas most definitely saw the beauty of his china. He saw his destiny in the apostles. He stared and stared and it all occurred to him, the only way I can get to my destiny is to sow into what I need. Barnabas said, "I need power, real power. I need to get to the nations." Truly the Lord said, "...It is more blessed to give than to receive". (Acts 20:35).

Barnabas knew that if he was obedient to the Spirit to sow into his destiny, that truly only God could give him what he needed. No man, only God. "And laid *them* down at the apostles' feet: and distribution was made unto every man according as he had need" (Acts 5:35). Barnabas knew that it was the Spirit that led him to sow his land into the anointing of the apostles. Therefore he was confident that the Lord would take care of all of his needs, not man.

It is the Spirit that does the distributing, beloved, not the apostles (man) only the Spirit of the Lord can do this. "....and distribution was made unto every man according as he had need" (Acts 4:35). Yes beloved, the Lord will make sure when you sow into any anointing, any ministry of the Lord, truly you will be blessed.

THE SPIRIT OF THE LORD SAITH SOW! SOW! SOW TO THE MINISTRY I AM LEADING YOU TO SOW! EVERY MAN NEED IS DIFFERENT, I WILL SUPPLY ALL YOUR NEEDS, EVERY MINISTRY SOW! EVERY CHURCH SOW! SOW INTO YOUR DESTINY. THIS IS THE WISDOM OF THE LORD!

"...These things saith-* he that is holy, he that is true, HE THAT HATH THE KEY OF DAVID, HE THAT OPENETH AND NO MAN SHUTTETH; AND SHUTTETH, AND NO MAN OPENETH;" (Rev. 3:7). Amen.

Chapter Twenty:
"Bless the Lord, O My Soul"

֍

"BLESS THE LORD, O MY SOUL: AND ALL THAT IS WITHIN ME, *BLESS* HIS HOLY NAME" (Ps. 103:1). Oh how often do we quote this particular Psalm? Isn't it just marvelous? Bless the Lord, O my soul: and all that is within me, bless his holy name.

Our heavenly Father wants his children to take this Psalm to the core of its meaning. One must be able to grasp the true essence of this Psalm. There is so much depth to this particular Psalm. Bless the Lord, O my soul. Here David (King David) is truly in the Spirit. And the Spirit will have him to bless the Lord of the most high (Jesus). Isn't this marvelous? All of this relies on the very truth, how we, God's people, by the Spirit, are to bless the Lord with our souls. How many times we have quoted this Psalm and prayed it? Nevertheless, the Spirit says there has to be depth and profound meaning of this particular Psalms, 103:1.

Oh beloved, all of the Psalms and the word is to be meditated and pondered over before we speak these precious words that belong to the Lord. That's right, beloved, this Psalm, 103:1, and all of God's word belongs to the Lord Jesus Christ. Why did David declare this in the Spirit? David declared this because he knew the word and God, our Father, were and are one. "In the beginning was the Word, and the Word was with God, and the Word was God. The same was in the beginning with God (John 1:1-2). David knew he had to be in a rightly position before he spoke the word of God. This rightly position would be pleasing in God's sight. Therefore, before he blessed the Lord with all his soul, David literally filtered every word before it was spoken. "LET THE WORDS OF MY MOUTH AND THE MEDITATION OF MY HEART, BE ACCEPTABLE IN THY SIGHT, O LORD, MY STRENGTH, AND MY REDEEMER" (Ps. 19:14). Here David is filtering every word before he blesses our heavenly Father by meditating on the word first, that comes out of his heart. At the end of this prayer David is encouraged by the Lord that when he is weak, or in need of redemption, our Lord God is his strength and redeemer.

O beloved, the Lord wants the same for us. Every word we bless the Lord with has to be filtered out by meditation upon the word that is in our hearts. If we do not consider this, the Lord will not receive our words, let alone our prayers. Empty words without depth and vague prayers do not minister to our heavenly Father. Meaningless words are vain and often times become repetitious.

The Pharisees questioned Jesus about his disciples not washing their hands before they ate. This very question would propose that Jesus own followers (his disciples) whom exemplified Jesus' righteousness, were not righteous at all. Jesus and his disciples did not follow the traditions of religious men. Jesus knew this was truly perversion and deception toward him and his disciples. Jesus response was "Well hath Isaiah prophesied of you hypocrites as it is written THIS PEOPLE HONOR ME WITH THEIR LIPS, BUT *THEIR* HEARTS IS FAR FROM ME. HOWBEIT IN VAIN DO THEY WORSHIP ME, TEACHING FOR DOCTRINES THE COMMANDMENTS OF MEN. For laying aside the commandment of God, ye hold the tradition of men, *as* the washing of pots and cups: and many other such like things ye do" (Mark 7:6-8).

This is crystal clear that Jesus is not referring this to his followers (disciples) or any of the brethren. But to the unbelievers that believe in the tradition of men and not of God "And he said unto them, Full well ye reject the commandment of God, that ye may keep your own tradition" (Mark 7:9). This beloved would be hypocrisy in the highest form. This is what happens when we speak words that are powerless or out of season. If we continue to just quote scriptures or have vague prayers, we will never reach our seasons.

You say, "What does one season have in reference to speaking God's word?" Time, time, time, beloved. If the word is not spoken in the right season, the word will not work for you. It will be null and void. You say, "We can call those things to be not as though they were." No beloved, every word must be spoken in the right

season and time. "TO EVERY *THING* THERE IS A SEASON, AND A TIME TO EVERY PURPOSE UNDER THE HEAVEN. A TIME TO REND, AND A TIME TO SOW, A TIME TO KEEP SILENCE, AND A TIME TO SPEAK" (Eccl. 3:1, 7). Yes beloved, confessing God's word is wonderful, as long as it's done by the Spirit. Without the Spirit the confession will not be fruitful because the season is barren. When we speak words that are unfruitful, we do not and can not bless God or his people. The season, the temperature, has to be perfect, even when blessing our heavenly Father. "BLESS THE LORD, O MY SOUL: AND ALL THAT IS WITHIN ME, *BLESS* HIS HOLY NAME"
(Ps.103:1). We can not just randomly bless the Lord; it comes out of our souls, out of our beings and out of our core. "…and all that is within me, bless his holy name."

David declares again, in the Spirit, "I WILL BLESS THE LORD AT ALL TIMES: HIS PRAISE *SHALL* CONTINUALLY BE IN MY MOUTH." The very next verse says, "MY SOUL SHALL MAKE HER BOAST IN THE LORD: THE HUMBLE SHALL HEAR *THEREOF*, AND BE GLAD" (Ps. 34:1-2). If the season is not right we can cause a lot of damage to God's people when we are making declarations and confessions. And we are not to confess them without the Spirit (the Spirit of God). God's people will be looking for these declarations, prophesies and confessions to come to pass. They will never come to pass if the Lord Jesus Christ did not move in your hearts to confess these words. The Lord Jesus Christ, by his Spirit, will tell you these confessions. He will make you to hear from the Spirit. I said, he will make you to hear them (the word) in the Spirit. Do not be dismayed that this will not apply to you. It most definitely will, trust him. Just like you trust him to wake you up every morning, put the same trust in him to speak to you every morning a word in season for God's people.

Isaiah the prophet knew this all too well. "The Lord God hath given me the tongue of the learned, that I should know how to speak a word in season to him that is weary: he wakeneth morning by morning, he wakeneth my ear to hear as the learned. The Lord God hath opened my ear, and I was not rebellious, neither turned away back" (Is. 50:4-5). Beloved, the Spirit says YOU DO NOT TURN BACK EITHER. DO NOT REBEL AGAINST

A SEASON WORD. RESIST THE TRADITION OF MEN BY CONFESSING UNFRUITFUL WORDS. DO NOT SPEAK WORDS THAT ARE UNPRODUCTIVE OR AIMLESS BUT SPEAK WORDS OF WISDOM AND COURAGE FOR I WILL QUICKEN YOUR SPIRIT TO DO SUCH A THING. DO NOT BE AFRAID. A SPOKEN WORD OUT OF SEASON IS LIKE A CANKER TO GOD'S PEOPLE. IT FESTERS TO NO END LEAVING GOD'S PEOPLE HELPLESS AND TOTALLY REJECTED. I SAY RESIST THE TEMPTATION OF YOUR OWN WORDS AND WORDS THAT ARE UNFRUITFUL. Even Jesus words were barren without the power behind them. "But if I cast out devils by the Spirit of God, then the kingdom of God is come unto you" (Matt 12:28). BLESS the Lord, O my soul and all that is within me, *bless* his holy name. The Spirit says THAT THE NEXT TIME YOU BLESS THE LORD WITH ALL YOUR SOUL AND EVERYTHING THAT IS WITHIN YOU, BLESS HIS HOLY NAME. REMEMBER THAT HIS HOLY NAME IS JESUS. AND JESUS NAME IS KEPT AND IS HOLY AS IS HIS WORD. So when you bless the Lord of the most high, it will not be in vain but by his Spirit.

"That we *henceforth* be no more children, tossed to and fro, and carried about with every wind of doctrine, by the slight of men, *and* cunning craftiness, whereby they lie and wait to deceive. But speaking the truth in love, may grow up into him in all things, which is the head, *even* Christ… Let no corrupt communication proceed out of your mouth, but that which is good to the use of edifying, that it may minister grace unto the hearers. And grieve not the holy Spirit of God, whereby ye are sealed unto the day of redemption. Let all bitterness, and wrath, and anger, and clamor, and evil speaking, be put away from you, with all malice: And be ye kind one to another, tender hearted, forgiving one another, even as God for Christ's sake hath forgiven you" (Eph. 4:14-15,29-32) Amen.

Chapter Twenty-One:
"Let Love Be Without Dissimulation"
Part I

❧

"Let love be without dissimulation..." (Rom 12:9). This particular word is for God's people. What a magnificent word from the Lord! Our Lord Jesus Christ loves you with a perfect love. The Lord is going to help you understand the true essence of the word, "Let love be without dissimulation..." (Rom. 12:9). You will be able to drink the sincere milk of the word.

"Let love be without dissimulation..." (Rom. 12:9). In order for one to understand this particular word, you must understand what the Lord is having you to see in the word dissimulation. Dissimulation is defined; making or becoming dissimilar. Dissimulation comes from the word dissimulate, which is defined; not similar or like, different. This is the key phrase, not similar or alike.

What is the Lord trying to tell you about dissimulation? The Lord wants you to know that love is love! Love has no dissimulation. Love has no difference. In other words, there is only one way to love. Love cannot and must not be without dissimulation. There is not anything to be compared to love. According to the word dissimulation, it is unlike or different than any other. This is the question unlike the other what? Anything and everything that is not love. Whatever comes to mind that is not love. Let love be without dissimulation. Love stands on its own unlike anything. Love is so powerful it also covers anything that is not love. "... And above all things, have fervent charity among yourselves for CHARITY COVERS A MULTITUDE OF SINS." (I Pet. 4:8).

The verse continues to say, "...Abhor that which is evil; and cleave to that which is good." (Rom. 12:9). Abhor is defined as: to shrink in fear, disgust, or hatred, detest, hate. This would be opposite of love. "We are to cleave (cling) to what is good. Cling to love. Forsake all evil. "Abstain from all appearances of evil. And the very God of peace sanctify you wholly..." (I. Thess. 5:22-23). Let love be without dissimulation.

The next verse declares, "Be kindly affectionate one to another with brotherly love; in honor preferring one another;" (Rom. 12:10). This verse is the epitome of showing love toward your brethren with kindness. Many times we say we love our fellow brethren but we stay clear of them or avoid them because of previous injuries or insults. This must not be. You must show affection to the other fellow brethren regardless. You cannot love or show kindness or affection at a distance. Reach out to the other brother or sister in love. Make a kind gesture toward them. This could be difficult for some of us because we have been wounded. The Lord knows this all too well. The solution is "And be ye kind one to another, tender hearted, forgiving one another, even as God for Christ sake hath forgiven you." (Eph. 4:32). Start regarding the other person or persons higher than yourselves. Yes, higher than yourselves, despite of the situation. This will fulfill this word, "... in honor preferring one another;" (Rom. 12:10).

The next verse continues, "Not slothful in business; fervent in spirit; serving the Lord;" (Rom. 12:11). This verse is not referring to your business, but indeed the Lord Jesus Christ and your heavenly Father's business. Whatever the Lord has ordained you to do, be not slothful (lazy) about what the Lord would have you to do for his kingdom. Whatever our heavenly Father has commanded your spirit to do be diligent (consistent) about it. In order for you to be fervent you have to be boiling over with anticipation and showing great intensity and devotion to the Lord Jesus Christ. This is pivotal (crucial). This ferventness and diligence must not be unto man, not even unto you. This ferventness must be in the spirit not the flesh. Although your flesh is doing most of the work, it is your spirit that wants to please the Lord Jesus Christ. The flesh must always be in subjection to your spirit. Your spirit must never be in subjection to your flesh. Your spirit man should be in control of your flesh. "So then they that are in the flesh cannot please God. But ye are not in the flesh, but in the Spirit, if so be that the Spirit of God dwell in you. Now if any man have not the Spirit of Christ, he is none of his." (Rom 8:8-10).

Therefore your spirit will always serve the Lord. And then this word will come to pass. "...fervent in spirit; serving the Lord;" (Rom. 12:11).

The next verse, "Rejoicing in hope; patient in tribulation; continuing instant in prayer;" (Rom. 12:12). These three are indeed one. The hope that we are to rejoice in is Jesus Christ. We are to continue to pray for his return and the tribulations that we encounter we must persevere with patience. Everyone has not come to the knowledge of Jesus Christ like we have. So be patient in tribulation and hold on to the promise of your soul. Rejoice, for Jesus is truly your anchor. "That by two immutable things, in which it was impossible for God to lie, we might have a strong consolation, who have fled for refuge to lay hold upon the hope set before us; Which hope we have an anchor of the soul, both sure and steadfast, which entereth into that without the veil; whither the forerunner is for us entereth, even Jesus, made a high priest forever after the order of Melchizedek" (Heb. 6:18-20).

This will be the sincere milk of the word, how marvelous. Our heavenly Father wants you to ponder on these verses, how you are to give yourselves over to this word from heaven for you. All of this word reflects on "love without dissimulation". No uncertain terms or misgivings, simply love. "Let love be without dissimulation..." (Rom.12:9).

Father we pray that you touch everyone that reads these letters. Keep them in your abiding presence forever. May the grace of our Lord Jesus Christ continue to be with you and the love of God, our Father. Amen.

Chapter Twenty-Two:
"Let Love Be Without Dissimulation"
Part II

❧

Oh how wonderful this is to let love be without dissimulation! (Rom. 12:9). Truly we ministered to you in the last letter about this particular word from our Lord Jesus Christ. How marvelous it is for our Heavenly Father to bless you with this wonderful word just for you.

We ministered to you before that the word dissimulation is defined, 'not similar or alike, different'. The Lord made this so clear that love is not like anything. The magnitude of love is powerful in itself. Nothing can be compared to it. Love completely stands on its own. Therefore, there can be nothing like it. You cannot divide love. Love is love. Let love be done without dissimulation. Let love be without difference. Let love be without dissimulation, no difference. Remember, you cannot divide love, the Spirit says, love is love. Therefore, you cannot say in your hearts that you love someone, but you do not like them or even their ways. How can this be? How can you love someone and turn about to say, "But I do not like this or these individuals?" How can you even say that you do not like their dispositions or personalities, but declare always that, "I still love them." This cannot be. We, the saints cannot say we love each other but detest a man's ways. Love is love. Let love be without dissimulation. Do not be deceived, little children.

The adversary would deceive your hearts to believe that it is perfectly well and good to have this sort of behavior. Well we tell you the truth, this behavior is not acceptable in the kingdom of God, nor is it acceptable in the land of the living (Earth). You cannot bless and curse at the same time. It has to be one or the other. You profess to love man and God and then turn around to say that I do not like or hate their ways. This cannot be. Oh little children, listen to what the Spirit of the Lord said by the apostle James, "Therewith bless we God, even the Father; and therewith curse we men, which are made after the similitude of God. Out of the same mouth proceedeth blessing and cursing. My brethren, these things ought not so to be. Doth a fountain sent forth at the same place sweet water and bitter? Can the fig tree, my brethren, bear olive berries? either a vine, figs? so can no fountain both yield salt water and fresh" (James 3:9-12).

You see beloved, it is impossible. Once you have grasped what the Lord is telling you about love then you will be able to exercise this commandment. Let love be without dissimulation.

"Among many of you," saith the Lord, "say that you love these people but indeed you loath their disposition." The Lord wants you to walk in the truth. It does not matter how you feel every time you see them. It does not matter what they say when they speak. It does not matter about their attire or appearance. It does not matter how they are. "Love is love", saith the Spirit of the Lord. No more my brethren. No more difference. If you love someone you just love them! Oh! Do not marvel, we tell you from here on you just love them. The next time these emotions rise up in you when you think or see them, remember that you just love them! Know this; these emotions are not from God. They are from your adversary. Therefore, you know these feelings about your brethren, or God's people, are not true. Hold on to the promised word. Let love be without dissimulation. Beloved, our whole walk is defeating the adversary. You have the victory! You must believe it.

A peace is shadowing you even as you read this letter. Many shall be delivered from bitterness, hatred and wrath. A peace shall overshadow you we say! This peace is the peace of God. This peace will keep your hearts by the love of God. And when these unclean thoughts about your brethren arise they will not prevail, because the peace is overshadowing now as you read! "And the peace of God, which passeth all understanding, shall keep your hearts and minds through Christ Jesus." (Phil l. 4:7).

Now that the Lord is blessing you with his peace about his people you now will be able to carry out the rest of his word. Oh you say, "but I am a child of God (a Christian). I love them but no one knows the pain and torment others have done to me, so how can I love that?" It is not you, beloved; it is God, your heavenly Father through Jesus Christ. This peace from God will guard your hearts if you let it. If you yield to the words of this letter, for you, even your worst adversary you will love and have great admiration for. Why? It's because you love them. You just love them. Let love be without dissimulation.

Oh dear children, this does not excuse the bad behavior of one's actions toward you. This is never acceptable. But what one does and how you feel are two different things. Righteousness and justice always persevere and wickedness and darkness never does. Our heavenly Father will repay all that was done to you. When the adversary would bring these people to mind, or have you in their presence that has wounded or persecuted you, do not fret, all is well. Many times the Lord requires us to invite the brethren to our homes. Oh, it is all so spiritual. And when we do we have to treat them the same as we would a long lost friend, with much love, giving, plenty of food and drink and plenty of love. "Distributing to the necessity of saints; given to hospitality. Bless them which persecute you: bless, and curse not" (Rom 12:13-14).

The Lord would have you to be mindful of these two verses, distributing (to divide, give out in shares) to the necessity of saints, given to hospital. As we stated there are times the Lord will have you make peace with the breaking of bread. We cannot curse these individuals who have wounded us, but indeed we bless them. Rom 12:17 continues to say "Recompense to no man evil for evil. Provide things honest in the sight of all men." There you have it. Always have good things accessible in their view. Always provide (give) these things that are wonderful in their sight. There is nothing more loving than a wonderful gift from the heart. No occasion, nothing special, just love. Just love. Let love be without dissimulation.

"If it be possible, as much as lieth in you, live peacefully with all men" (Rom. 12:18). Now you say, "I could never do this. I could never live peacefully with all men." Oh dear children, you cannot on your own. It is simply according to the word "... as much as lieth in you". This is what waits inside of you. What awaits or lieth in you? It is Jesus. Dear beloved, it is Jesus that lieth in you. Is it possible? Will you let Christ in you love and be at peace with all men? "To whom God would make known what is the riches of the glory of this mystery among the Gentiles; which is Christ in you, and the hope of glory:" (Col. 1:27). This would be the only way to live peacefully with all men. To Jesus be all the glory. Amen.

Beloved, you do not have to seek revenge unto those who has persecuted you. God, your heavenly Father will do it his way not your way. "Dearly beloved, avenge not yourselves, but rather give place unto wrath: for it is written, VENGEANCE IS MINE; I WILL REPAY, saith the Lord" (Rom. 12:19). The next time the adversary tries to take over your thoughts and you start to have animosity over God's people, remember, let love be without dissimulation.

"Therefore, IF THINE ENEMY HUNGER, FEED HIM; IF HE THIRST, GIVE HIM DRINK: FOR IN SO DOING THOU SHALT HEAP COALS OF FIRE ON HIS HEAD. Be not overcome of evil, but overcome evil with good" (Rom. 12:20-21). There, all is well beloved. You now will be able to fulfill all of this word by simply not dividing love. Let love be without dissimulation.

We know many of you have been set free from bitterness and wrath. The Spirit of peace is still overshadowing you as we write to you with much love and the anticipation of the fruit you are going to bear unto God.

Father God we pray that the love of Jesus Christ, himself, will keep your people. We speak a blessing to you and your entire families and ministries. We pray, dear Jesus that every sickness will leave their bodies as we command it to go in Jesus name! "Wherefore lift up the hands which hang down, and the feeble knees; And make straight paths for your feet, lest that which is lame be turned out of the way; but let it rather be healed" (Heb. 12:12-13). Oh rejoice, rejoice, rise and walk. Let the blind see and the deaf hear and the lame walk! Do what you could not do before! We commend it to be in Jesus name!

We know many of you were healed by the love of God in his Son Jesus Christ.

May the grace of our Lord Jesus Christ continue to be with you and the love of God, our Father. Amen.

Chapter Twenty-Three:
"But Ye Are a Chosen Generation:
Part I

⟳

"But ye are a chosen generation, a royal priesthood, an holy nation a peculiar people; that ye should shew forth the praises of him who hath called you out of darkness into his marvelous light"(I Pet. 2:9). There you have it, how wonderful is this! Oh precious saints that God our heavenly Father has done all these wonderful things just for us. It is so marvelous for your Lord Jesus Christ and our Father God to behold us in such a manor. What a privilege and an incredible honor for our maker to look upon us with such a beautiful overview.

This very word was an incredible prophecy indeed to the very first fruit of the Spirit (Israel). Oh yes saints, Israel. Israel is and always will be the first fruit of the Spirit. "YE HAVE SEEN WHAT I DID UNTO THE EGYPTIANS, AND *HOW* I BARE YOU ON EAGLES' WINGS, AND BROUGHT YOU UNTO MYSELF. NOW THEREFORE, IF YOU WILL OBEY MY VOICE INDEED, AND KEEP MY COVENANT, THEN YE SHALL BE A PECULIAR TREASURE UNTO ME ABOVE ALL PEOPLE: FOR ALL THE EARTH IS MINE. AND YE SHALL BE UNTO ME, A KINGDOM OF PRIESTS, AND A HOLY NATION. THESE *ARE* THE WORDS WHICH THOU SHALT SPEAK UNTO THE CHILDREN OF ISRAEL" (Ex. 19:4-6). When our heavenly Father birth something (that is to bring forth) it will always be his first fruit. Everything that our heavenly Father does, he does it by his Spirit. Therefore, anything that our heavenly Father does the first time will be considered the first fruits of the Spirit. Israel is the first fruit of the Spirit. Even chronologically and historically we see that Israel was and still is the first fruit of God.

Deliverance came to them first by the way of Moses and when God himself manifested his word on earth (Jesus) who became flesh then salvation was offered to the Jews first and then the Gentiles. "Jesus said unto her, Woman, believe me, that the hour cometh, when ye shall neither in this mountain, or yet at Jerusalem, worship the Father. Ye worship ye know not what we know what we worship: for salvation is of the Jews (John 4:21-22). How wonderful salvation is of the Jews first (first fruits). ISRAEL *WAS* THE HOLINESS UNTO THE LORD, *AND* THE FIRST FRUITS OF HIS INCREASE..." (Jer. 2:3).

Oh beloved, there is nothing to be desirous about. We have the same right as Israel the Jews. There is no difference for us. Something has to be birth first then it shall yield a beautiful thing. The same blessing is for you the (Gentiles). "For we know that the whole creation groaneth and travaileth in pain together until now. And not only *they*, but ourselves also, which hath the first fruits of the Spirit, even we ourselves groan within ourselves, waiting for the adoption, *to wit*, the redemption of our body (Rom. 8:22-23). There you see, not only they but ourselves also. It does not matter what nationality or people we are, as long as you are in Christ Jesus, you will fulfill salvation. Yes beloved, they as in (Israel the Jews). Those who have called on the name of the Lord are now in Christ Jesus. "For whosoever shall call upon the name of the Lord shall be saved" (Rom. 10:13). Hallelujah. Amen.

There you have it. There is no reason to feel inadequate or unsafe, not even jealous. Your heavenly Father, God almighty loves all his children that are called unto him by Christ Jesus. "But ye are a chosen generation, a royal priesthood, an holy nation, a peculiar people; that ye should shew forth the praises of him who hath called you out of darkness into his marvelous light" (I. Pet 2:9). This prophetic word was and is for Israel and for you. You must believe this. The promises that you're heavenly Father have for Israel are for you too by his Son Jesus Christ. God's only Son just for you. "For God so loved the world: that he gave his only begotten Son, that whosoever believeth on him should not perish, but have everlasting life" (John 3:16). Oh how God, your heavenly Father, loves you with a perfect love.

Many of you are complex about Israel the Jews. The Lord would have you to take a deep breath concerning this. The Lord knows how to separate, put together and orchestrate his people. Some of you believe that salvation indeed, is not for the Jews. This is not how salvation works. It is for all men who come to the truth. God has not forsaken his first fruits. This is what Paul said who experienced the same matter. "I say then, Hath God cast away his people? God forbid. For I also am an Israelite, of the seed of Abraham, *of* the tribe of Benjamin. God hath not cast away his people which he foreknew. Wot ye not what the scripture saideth of Elias? how he maketh intercession to God to Israel saying, Lord, they have killed thy prophets, and digged down thine alters; and I am left alone, and they seek my life. But what saideth the answer of God unto him? I have reserved to myself seven thousand men, who have not bowed the knee to *the image of* Baal. Even so then at this present time also there is a remnant according to the election of grace" (Rom 11:1-5).

You see, God knows exactly what he is doing. You have no need to feel insecure of another people or nation. There was a time when men actually prayed against Israel. Even now they still do. You are not to make intercession to God about prevention of salvation to a people or nation. Salvation is from the Lord. You say, "I have never done such a thing." Beloved, every time you say in your heart that salvation is not for the Jews because they do not know the Lord, you have prayed that prayer....I A M THE LORD GOD OF HEAVEN AND EARTH AND I HEAR ALL THINGS AND I KNOW ALL THINGS. IT IS NOT WHOLESOME FOR YOU TO BLASPHEMINE A NATION THAT IS CALLED MY PEOPLE. I AM THE LORD GOD, YOU MUST REPENT OF ALL THESE UNCLEAN THOUGHTS. SALVATION IS FROM THE LORD YOUR GOD, NOT MEN. SALVATION DOES NOT BELONG TO ANY MAN, BUT UNTO GOD, YOUR HEAVENLY FATHER. AND WHEN SALVATION COMES IT COMES WITH A WONDERFUL PACKAGE, IT IS CALLED A BLESSING. OH HOW MARVELOUS! A BLESSING, SALVATION NEVER COMES ALONE. IT IS IN THE BLESSING, BELOVED. I SAY IT IS IN THE BLESSING BELOVED WHEN YOU RECEIVE ALL OF SALVATION. IT IS NOT JUST FOR YOU BUT FOR ALL MEN THAT WILL COME UNTO ME. ALL I CALL THAT COME UNTO ME SHALL RECEIVE SALVATION WITH THE MARVELOUS PACKAGE (BLESSINGS). BELOVED, CAN YOU EVEN NUMBER

THE TIMES I HAVE BLESSED YOU? START TO NUMBER. GO RIGHT AHEAD, BELOVED, START TO NUMBER. IT IS NOT POSSIBLE I SAY, IT IS NOT POSSIBLE FOR THOSE OF YOU WHO HAVE SALVATION TO NUMBER TIMES THAT I HAVE BLESSED YOU! AS THE STARS ARE IN THE HEAVENS AND THE GRAINS IN THE SAND SO ARE MY BLESSINGS UPON YOU. "EVEN DAVID DECLARED, " I WILL PRAISE THEE; FOR I AM FEARFULLY *AND* WONDERFULLY MADE: MARVELOUS *ARE* THY WORKS; AND *THAT* MY SOUL KNOWETH RIGHT WELL. MY SUBSTANCE WAS NOT HID FROM THEE, WHEN I WAS MADE IN SECRET, *AND* CURIOUSLY WROUGHT IN THE LOWEST PARTS OF THE EARTH. THINE EYES DID SEE MY SUBSTANCE, YET BEING UNPERFECT; AND IN THY BOOK ALL *MY MEMBERS* WERE WRITTEN, *WHICH* IN CONTINUANCE WERE FASHIONED, WHEN *AS YET THERE WAS* NONE OF THEM. HOW PRECIOUS ALSO ARE THY THOUGHTS UNTO ME, O GOD! HOW GREAT IS THE SUM OF THEM! *IF* I SHOULD COUNT THEM, THEY ARE MORE IN NUMBER THAN THE SAND: WHEN I WAKE, I AM STILL WITH THEE" (Ps. 139:14-18)

Never try and stop this wonderful thing called salvation from another people or another nation. Salvation is for all men. I say all men, with a wonderful package, the blessing. "SALVATION *BELONGETH* UNTO THE LORD: THY BLESSING IS UPON THY PEOPLE. SELAH" (Ps. 3:8). "But ye are a chosen generation, a royal priesthood, an holy nation, a peculiar people; that ye should shew forth the praises of him who hath called you out of darkness into his marvelous light" (I Pet. 2:9). We will stop here, beloved, until next month.

Father God, we pray that you bless every partner of Helen Trower Ministries and all of your people throughout every generation. Continue to keep us and bless us by your abiding power. Father we pray that every nation will answer your call through Jesus Christ. Forgive us, for we know not what we do or say. Search our hearts, O God. We are earnestly sorry that we thought or prayed these unclean thoughts for we truly repent of these sins. For we are all your people in Christ Jesus. We love you Lord. We thank you for shedding your precious blood for our sins. Thank you Father for the cleansing of your Son Jesus

Christ's precious blood. We thank you Lord, we thank you again for shedding your precious blood for our sins. We thank you Father that we are white as snow because of the precious blood of Jesus Christ that was shed for all men. "And from Jesus Christ who is the faithful witness, and the first begotten of the dead, and the prince of the kings of the earth. Unto him that loved us, and washed us from our sins in his own blood. And have made us kings and priests unto God and his father; to him be the glory and dominion forever and ever, Amen" (Rev. 1:5-6).

Chapter Twenty-Four:
"But Ye Are a Chosen Generation: Part II

∾

"But ye are a chosen generation, a royal priesthood, an holy nation, a peculiar people; that ye should shew forth the praises of him who hath called out of darkness into his marvelous light:" (I Pet. 2:9). This blessed word from the Lord is so wonderful. The Lord would have us to continue about his blessing toward his people. The last month we ministered to you about salvation belonged to all men in Christ Jesus. Only in Christ Jesus does salvation belong to men. One must accept what our Savior, Jesus Christ, has done, not only for us but for the whole world. "And he is the propitiation for our sins: and not for ours only, but also for the *sins* of the whole world" (I John 2:2).

Many of you are still complex about the Jews' (Israel) faith where the Lord Jesus Christ is concerned. The Lord knows who belongs to him. There is not one soul who will not get into the kingdom without or through Jesus Christ. All men have to come to the repentance of their sins and confess with their mouths and believe in their hearts that Jesus Christ was raised from the dead. "But what saith it? The word is nigh thee, *even* in thy mouth, and in thy heart: that is, the word of faith, which we preach; That if thou shall confess with thou mouth the Lord Jesus, and shall believe in thine heart that God has raised him from the dead, thou shall be saved. For with the heart man believeth unto righteousness; and with the mouth confession is made unto salvation. For the scripture saith, Whosoever believeth on him shall not be ashamed. For there is no difference between the Jew and the Greek: for the same Lord over all is rich unto all that call upon him. For whosoever shall call upon the name of the Lord shall be saved" (Rom 10:8-13).

This is just wonderful! How marvelous is this...that the same Lord is rich unto all that call upon him. Rich is defined, having more than enough, having abundance, well supplied, abounding, worth much, valuable, costly, having abundance of good constituents or qualities full of strength, deep, plentiful, ample. Yes beloved, the Lord Jesus Christ is rich unto all that call upon him. There is plenty enough salvation for all men not just for certain people or a nation. This is all so marvelous! O how we bless your holy name, Lord Jesus!

Now beloved, do not say in your hearts who salvation is for. Salvation is for the Jews and the Gentiles. You being Gentiles know all too well according the scriptures how salvation was sent to the Gentiles through God's servant. Nevertheless the servant of the Lord, who was a Jew, also felt and feel the way many Gentiles do this day about Jews. "NOW THE WORD OF THE LORD CAME UNTO JONAH THE SON OF AMITTAI SAYING. ARISE, GO TO NINEVEH, THAT GREAT CITY, AND CRY AGAINST IT; FOR THEIR WICKEDNESS IS COME UP BEFORE ME. BUT JONAH ROSE UP TO FLEE UNTO TARSHISH FROM THE PRESENCE OF THE LORD, AND WENT DOWN TO JOPPA AND HE FOUND A SHIP GOING TO TARSHISH: SO HE PAID THE FAIR THEREOF, AND WENT DOWN INTO IT, TO GO WITH THEM UNTO TARSHISH FROM THE PRESENCE OF THE LORD" (Jonah 1:1-3).

Jonah fled (ran) from the presence of the Lord before he would preach to Nineveh, which he considered to be God's enemies. Jonah felt all the sin that this people had committed was useless. Jonah believed that God's salvation was not (rich) enough or plenteous enough for this group of people, Gentiles. But God is (rich) abundant in salvation had more than enough. Sometimes we feel or believe that one's sins are so awful that salvation can not handle it or that salvation cannot even perhaps save that soul. Well we tell you the truth and no lie, salvation is rich. Jesus Christ is rich in his salvation. Salvation is more than enough. Oh how Jonah came to believe and underestimated that salvation is not minimized or contained by the wisdom of men. But salvation is of the Lord.

When Jonah was praying and interceding on the behalf of Nineveh trying to convince the Lord about their sins this was the conclusion of Jonah's prayer, "WHEN MY SOUL FAINTED WITHIN ME I REMEMBERED THE LORD: AND MY PRAYER CAME IN UNTO THEE, INTO THINE HOLY TEMPLE. THEY THAT OBSERVED LYING VANITIES FORSAKE THEIR OWN MERCY. BUT I WILL SACRIFICE UNTO THEE WITH THE VOICE OF THANKSGIVING: I WILL PAY *THAT* THAT I HAVE VOWED. SALVATION IS OF THE LORD. AND THE LORD SPAKE UNTO THE FISH, AND IT VOMITED OUT JO' NAH UPON THE DRY *LAND"* (Jonah 2: 7-10).

You see beloved, Jonah came to the realization that salvation belonged to the Lord, not him or even you, but the Lord God almighty. Many of you are in a situation where you need to be vomited out on dry land. You are in a battle within yourselves about God's people. Salvation is of the Lord and leave it there.

Peter, Jesus' apostle, also struggled with the same situation. Peter was told also to go and preach to the Gentiles. He also felt the way Jonah did. Nevertheless, Peter, like Jonah, was also obedient. Peter was sent by the Lord Jesus Christ and his Holy Spirit to preach to a certain man in Caesarea called Cornelius, a centurion of the band called the Italian *band.* Peter went and preached to Cornelius and his whole household this glorious message from the living God. "Then Peter opened *his* mouth and said, of a truth I perceive that God is no respecter of persons: But in every nation he that feareth him, and worketh righteousness, is accepted with him. The word which *God* sent unto the children of Israel, preaching peace by Jesus Christ: (he is Lord of all:) That word, *I say,* ye know, which was published throughout all Judea, and begin from Galilee, after the baptism which John preached; How God anointed Jesus of Nazareth with the Holy Ghost and with power: who went about doing good, and healing all that were oppressed of the devil; for God was with him. And we are witnesses of all things which he did both in the land of the Jews, and in Jerusalem; whom they slew and hang on a tree: Him God raised up the third day, and shewed him openly; Not to all the people; but unto witnesses chosen before of God, *even* to us, who did eat and drink with him after he rose from the dead. And he commandeth us to preach unto the people and to testify that it is he which was ordained of God *to be* the Judge of the quick and the dead. To him give all the prophets witness, that through his name whosever believeth in him shall receive remission of sins. While Peter yet spake these words, the Holy Ghost fell on all them which heard the word. And they of the circumcision which believed were astonished, as many as came with Peter, because that on the Gentiles also was poured out the gift of the Holy Ghost. For they heard them speak with tongues and magnify God. Then answered Peter, Can any man forbid water, that these should not be baptized, which hath received the Holy Ghost as well as we? And he commandeth them to be baptized in the name of the Lord. Then prayed they him to tarry certain days" (Acts 10: 34-48).

In the name of Jesus Christ we command every believer, every Gentile, everyone that believeth on the name Jesus Christ to receive ye the Holy Ghost! As the Spirit of the Lord is pouring out over you now start to magnify (praise) God with the utterance of speaking with tongues Just start magnifying him and let this gift of God flow through you because truly the Spirit of the Lord is there with you and has given you this gift. Praise the Lord, you have been baptized with the Holy Ghost! We thank God for your baptism and your salvation. What a glorious time this is. Rejoice in the Lord!

And we pray God to hear from you soon with your marvelous testimonies to Jesus be all the glory and praise. "And it shall come to pass in the last days, saith God, I will pour out my Spirit upon all flesh: and your sons and your daughters shall prophesy and your young men shall see visions, and your old men shall dream dreams" (Acts 2:17). Amen.

Chapter Twenty- Five:
"Rejoice in the Lord Always"

❧

Grace and peace from God our Father and his Son Jesus Christ. We write to you with much love and joy in Christ Jesus for we know that your rewards are laid up for you in heaven with your inheritance in Christ Jesus. For we thank God for your labor in Christ Jesus.

"Rejoice in the Lord alway: *and* again I say rejoice" (Phil. 4:4). Oh how wonderful this word from the Lord is. So wonderfully rich in the fullness of Jesus Christ. Rejoicing in the Lord is a marvelous thing. The Lord would want you to rejoice in him so much that all believers, all doubtful, all of those who draw back, will come back to him. There is so much pleasure, good pleasure in this. Your heavenly Father has much pleasure when we draw near to him and rejoice. "Now the just shall live by faith: but if *any ma*n draw back, my soul shall have no pleasure in him. But we are not of them who draw back unto perdition; but of them that believe to the saving of the soul" (Heb. 10:39).

You see, beloved, we must not draw back. If we do our Lord God will not have any pleasure in what we do or say, let alone have pleasure in us. Oh beloved, how our heavenly Father wants to bless you. It is in his pleasure for us that brings out such wonderful rewards, fruits and beautiful works. These beautiful rewards and beautiful works were put in you before the foundation of earth was laid down. Oh how marvelous this is. "For it is God which worketh in you both to will and to do of *his* good pleasure" (Phil. 2:13). Now that is something to rejoice about beloved! You need not to fret about ever getting out of God's will or feeling inadequate about anything. Everything that your heavenly Father purpose in you was laid down and designed just for you.

This foundation that he laid down is in his Son Christ Jesus. REJOICE! Everything that our heavenly Father purpose for your lives is in Christ Jesus. Hallelujah! Oh how marvelous. You do not have to look for it, stop trying to search out your identity. Your identity is in Christ Jesus. Every purpose that your heavenly Father put in you can only be released through Christ Jesus. "According as he has chosen us in him before the foundation of the world, that we should be holy and without blame before him in love: Having predestinated us into the adoption of children by Jesus Christ to himself, according to the good pleasure of his will, To the praise of the glory of his grace, wherein he hath made us accepted in the beloved. In whom we have redemption through his blood, the forgiveness of sins, according to the riches of his grace; Wherein he hath abounded toward us in all wisdom and prudence; Having made known unto us the mystery of his will, according to his good pleasure which he hath purposed in himself: That any dispensation of the fulness of times he might gather together in one all things in Christ, both which are in heaven, and which are on earth; *even* in him: in whom also we have obtained an inheritance, being predestinated according to the purpose of him who worketh all things after the council of his own will: That we should be to the praise of his glory, who first trusted in Christ" (I Eph.1:4-12).

This is it beloved… who first trusted in Christ. Paul makes it vividly clear that one must first trust in Christ before he can even obtain these precious things that belongs to God in you, yes in you!

Paul just stated earlier that, "… God which worketh in you both to will and to do of *his* good pleasure" (Phil. 2 :13). God is constantly working things out in you. REJOICE! Your heavenly Father has put something very valuable inside of you. It was placed inside of you before you were even born. This would be the purpose of God in your life. This beautiful thing which is God's purpose was placed in you, inside your mother's womb. When we were conceived this establishment was in the Spirit. The almighty God placed his hand on your mother's womb and separated (consecrated) you unto himself through Christ Jesus. This is

God's ordained purpose in your life. "BEFORE I FORMED THEE IN THE BELLY, I KNEW THEE; AND BEFORE THOUGH CAMEST FORTH OUT OF THE WOMB I SANCTIFIED THEE,

AND I ORDAINED THEE A PROPHET UNTO THE NATIONS"
(Jer. 1:5). REJOICE, I SAY REJOICE!

This is marvelous. You only have to realize that the foundation
of Jesus Christ was laid down for you oh so long ago! God purpose
through his Son is inside of you. Beloved, consider yourself as a
holding place. A place that holds and contains your heavenly
Father's wonderful works. "But we have this treasure in earthen
vessels, that the excellency of the power may be of God, and not of
us" (II Cor. 4:7). This is so wonderful. We are all in Christ Jesus.

This beloved you know all so well.

As we stir up your remembrance you will start to remember
the actual ordination (the consecration). This is all so spiritual. But
the Spirit will reveal these depths of God through Christ Jesus.
"But as it is written, Eye have not seen, nor ear heard, neither
have entered into the heart of man, the things which God hath
prepared for them who love him. But God hath revealed *them*
unto us by his Spirit: for the Spirit searcheth all things, yea, the
deep things of God" (I Cor. 2:9-10). You see beloved God reveals to
us these things by his Spirit. The Spirit searcheth for depths (deep
things) of God and reveals them to us by Christ Jesus. "Howbeit
when he cometh the Spirit of truth, is come, he will guide you into
all truth: for he shall not speak of himself; but whatsoever he shall
hear, *that* shall he speak: and he will shew you things to come. He
shall glorify me: for he shall receive a mind, and shew *it* unto you.
All things that the Father hath are mine: therefore said I that he
shall take of mine, and shall shew it unto you" (John 16:13-15).

It is by Jesus that the Spirit does the revealing. God always
shows us new things before it comes forth, this is his nature.
"BEHOLD, THE FORMER THINGS ARE COME TO PASS, AND
NEW THINGS DO I DECLARE: BEFORE THEY SPRING FORTH
I TELL YOU OF THEM" (Is. 42:9). The Lord always reveals things
to us by his Spirit. Consecration to him is very rare. It is not in
all men that God has his purpose. It is only in those who are
sacrificially obedient and simply adore and have a genuine love
for him and the brethren. These are the elect whom he has chosen
to do his will. You see God can not trust everyone with his will
but those of you who he has chosen you truly need to REJOICE!

I come to you in the name of Jesus Christ, Lord reveal to every
servant your purpose that dwells in them. Lord consecrate every

servant holy unto yourself . Stir up the remembrance of all the initial callings, stir up the remembrance to their first calling in you (Christ Jesus). Let us serve you with vigor and tenacity. Let it be. THE SPIRIT OF THE LORD SAYETH, BE NOT SLACK IN YOUR LORD JESUS, BE NOT SLACK WASTE NO TIME. I SAY WASTE NO TIME- HE IS ABOUT TO RISE LET GOD BE TRUE AND EVERY MAN A LIAR GO I SAY TO YOUR OWN COURTS, MAKE MENTION TO THAT NAME JESUS, JESUS, POSITION YOURSELVES IN YOUR OWN COURTS, GO TO YOUR POST I SAY GO THAT IS WHERE YOU WILL FIND ME. I SHOW YOU ALL THINGS, AGAIN, AGAIN- NOW REMEMBER THE OLD SO YOU CAN DO THE NEW. REMEMBER WHAT I FIRST TOLD YOU. REMEMBER WHAT WE FIRST SPOKE TO YOU. PERFORM YOUR DUTY. FOR YOUR STEWARDHOOD TO JESUS IS VITAL, THE LORD IS AT HAND. I TAKE YOU BACK- I STIR YOU UP IN REMEMBRANCE HOW TO GO FORTH AND COMPLETE THE WORK THAT OUR JESUS GAVE TO YOU. I SAY DO NOT SLACK GO FORWARD WITH THE PURPOSE THAT JESUS ORDAINED YOU TO DO. YOU ARE CHOSEN! REJOICE!

"And we know that all things work together for good to them that love God, to them who are the called according to his purpose. For whom he did foreknow, he also did predestinate *to be* conformed to the image of his Son, that he might be the first born among many brethren. Moreover whom he did predestinate, them he also called: and whom he called, them he also justified, in whom it justified, them he also glorified" (Rom. 8:28-30). ~Amen

Chapter Twenty-Six:
"Weeping May Endure for a Night"

❧

It has been said, "...weeping may endure for a night, but joy *cometh* in the morning" (Ps. 30:5). How endearing that after one goes through a season of weeping there is much joy afterward. Yes beloved, there are seasons of weeping. Weeping come to refresh and restore. Weeping is a must for the beloved saints of God. O how wonderful this! It is all so marvelous that we are to discover that weeping is a seasonal session, yes, a session. The beloved saints have and will always go through, a season or session of weeping. Weeping always equips the saints for what is to come. One must go through a season of weeping. Yes beloved, every saint must go through this season of weeping. We tell you the truth, weeping is seasonal, weeping is seasonal. "...weeping may endure for a night, but joy *cometh* in the morning" (Ps. 30:5).

David hear is speaking about a season of weeping. David is speaking in the Spirit. "...weeping my endure for a night, but joy *cometh* in the morning" (Ps. 30:5). David was not talking about the night as we know it. Our heavenly Father wants his beloved to have an understanding about the night that he is speaking about. This night is not the period from sunset to sunrise or the period of darkness after sunset and before sunrise. This would be the norm for all creation. This would be the expectancy. But what we do not expect is a night season. This is the season that weeping enters. Yes beloved, a night season. This is so marvelous!

You see weeping comes in seasons. This season would be the night season. The night that our heavenly Father wants us to grasp is not when you lay your head down to sleep, but a season or period we go through. It is like a session. We say session because sessions can be long and sporadic. A session is defined, a period of activity of any kind. This is why the Lord is saying *like* a session. For when we go through this season of the night period, it will feel and appear as a session. Remember the night that David speaks of here is seasonal.

Weeping is seasonal. The season is night. It has been this way from the beginning. "While the earth remained, seed time and harvest, and cold and heat, and summer and winter, and day and night shall not cease" (Gen. 8:22). Yes beloved, here our heavenly Father speaks of seedtime, which is seasonal, the harvest which is seasonal, the cold which is seasonal, and the heat which is seasonal and the summer which is seasonal, and the winter which is seasonal, and the day which is seasonal, and last the night, which is seasonal. All of these come in their own seasons. But what we do not realize is that day and night are seasons. One of the definitions of night is any period or condition of darkness or gloom. This is what David here is speaking of, a spiritual darkness, the night season. "...weeping may endure for a night, but joy *cometh* in the morning" (Ps. 30:5). Now beloved, you have grasped the true meaning of this scripture.

The entire body of Jesus Christ is going through a night season. As the Lord himself takes you through this night season, we pray and know that you will come out with joy. Our heavenly Father wants to ensure you that your weeping may endure for a night but your joy is coming in the morning. Many of the saints are weeping now in private because you do not want the world to know that you are sorrowful and despair, let alone weeping. Many of the saints have gone from prominent to a lowly state, prosperity-wise and spiritual. You are reaching out to God but you still somehow feel as though he is not there or responding to your cries. All of the calamity with the decline of what you once knew as prosperity has left some of you. Therefore, you are in a season of weeping, gloom, darkness (night). O, but do not be sure of yourselves beloved. Do not rely on your emotions or even your current situation. We say again, do not rely on what you see, do not trust it. Our heavenly Father wants you to trust not in oppression but in his word. If you can not, because of all of the despair and calamity around you, we beseech you, beloved, trust in his word. After all, the word is for you, just for you. Trust in his word. Isaiah said, " The grass withered, the flower fadeth: but the word of our God shall stand forever" (Is. 40:8). If something stand forever this is worth trusting in. Trust in his word beloved.

David prophesied about this weeping period we, the saints, are going through in Psalms 30. This weeping period, the night season, has always been in existence. David speaks about this very retrospectively and prophetically. In retrospect, David speaks about his seasons along with Israel. And then he prophesied about the church, which is us. David makes it vividly clear that this night season that we the saints are weeping, about is normally after some sort of loss or tragedy. Especially when it comes to our prosperity. When our prosperity has been removed it will take a great toll on, we, the saints. Why? Because we do not know anything else but how to be blessed and victorious. This is how we were molded and shaped from the beginning to the end. You, the saints, are the most prosperous and powerful people on the earth. You always have been and you always will be. This is a prayer that was prayed over the saints so long ago by our beloved brethren John. "Beloved, I wish above all things that thou mayest prosper and be in health, even as thy soul prospereth" (III John 1:2). So to temporarily lose this prosperity, we say temporary, it can be devastating to some of you. Prosperity is our nature. We the saints do not know how to live without it. We are blessed indeed. "Salvation *belongeth* unto the Lord: thy blessing *is* upon thy people. Se'lah" (Ps. 3:8).

David continues to say here in retrospect and prophetically in Psalms 30 about how he and we will lose our prosperity temporarily. He speaks about how he and we believe that we could never be moved our touched by any circumstances. Although circumstances come but surely it will not touch me, David declares. This would be impossible. I will not be touched and my prosperity will never leave me physically or spiritually. David said, "...weeping may endure for a night, but joy *cometh* in the morning. And in my prosperity I said, I shall never be moved" (Ps. 30:5-6). You see David is so apparent and to the point. He hides nothing from our heavenly Father, nothing, "...in my prosperity I said I shall never be moved" (Ps. 30:6). Well, many of the saints have said the same thing. Only because we know and trust his word. And we know that we are blessed and God has created everything on this earth for we, the saints. "For the earnest expectation of the creature waiteth for the manifestation of the sons of God. For the creature was made subject to vanity, not willingly, but by reason of him who hath subjected *the same* in hope, Because the creature itself shall also be delivered from the bondage of corruption into the glorious liberty of the children of God" (Rom. 8:19-21).

So how can this be, we say? The Lord has always been there for me, always. But somehow I am not for certain that he is there now. This echoes in many of the saints hearts. David continued to say, "Lord, by thy favor thou hast made my mountain to stand strong: thou didst hide thy face, *and* I was troubled (Ps. 30:7). David said, "...and I was troubled"(Ps. 30:7). This is the night season that David was going through and now we the church. Some of you are weeping physical tears. Others are lamenting for some spiritual cause. Nevertheless, weeping is defined to cry; complain, to manifest or give expression to a strong emotion, usually grief or sorrow, by crying, whaling or esp. shedding tears, to lament or morn. This weeping in the night is a turning point for all believers. It is his word. Israel felt troubled. The church is troubled. The Lord sees all of your tears in this night season. For you must shed your tears. But dear children, you must also give thanks to God in all things. "In everything give thanks: for this is the will of God in Christ Jesus concerning you" (I. Thes. 5:18).

As difficult as it is to give God thanks through Jesus Christ for your weeping, your tears are so valuable, your tears are powerful! Without the weeping the Lord can not give you this incredible gift of joy. Your tears are your substance. David in the Spirit said again in another Psalms, "The Lord hath done great things for us: *whereof* we are glad. Turn again our captivity, O Lord, as the streams in the south. They that sow in tears shall reap in joy. He that goeth forth and weepeth, bearing precious seed shall doubtless come again with rejoicing, bringing his sheaves *with him*. (Ps. 126:3-6). Do not forget what your heavenly Father has done for you through Jesus Christ our Lord. You must continue to give thanks to the Father through Jesus Christ.

Jesus is key to everything beloved. You must go through Jesus. "...I am the way, the truth, and the life: no man cometh unto the Father, but by me" (John 14:6). Jesus is the key, even when we are giving thanks to our heavenly Father. You must give thanks to God, beloved, in this night season. Then you will begin to see the joy bearing your precious seed. It is all so marvelous! Giving thanks to God during this night season of weeping is difficult, but being mindful that we believers must have hope and trust in God's word. You then will be able to see your faith come alive. Faith is activated by belief. "Now faith is the substance of things hoped for, the evidence of things not seen" (Heb. 11:1).

You must believe and trust in God's word. When you give thanks to God, even in this night season, your joy will come. Do not wait too long to give thanks and praises to him. Do it while you are alive. It will not profit you any other way. David continued to say in Psalms 30, " I cried to thee, O Lord; and unto the Lord I made supplication. What prophet *is there* in my blood, when I go down to the pit? Shall the dust praise thee? shall it declare thy truth. Hear, O Lord, and have mercy upon me: Lord, be thou my helper" (Ps. 30:8-10). Here David is reminded that he, and we, should give thanks right now while we are still breathing (alive). And when we do this a miracle will happen...all of a sudden everything has changed. Our prosperity has returned, our mountain is standing strong again. And then comes the incredible joy that we told you about. " ...weeping may endure for a night, but joy *cometh* in the morning" (day) that other season in Genesis 8:22. Hallelujah!

We, the saints, are waiting for the morning, the day season. There you have it, beloved, joy cometh in the morning. Oh how glorious is this! Can you feel the morning coming? Can you feel the sun? It is about to come up. Do you feel the heat of the day, that glorious other season, the heat? That other wonderful season in Genesis 8:22. Can you feel it? Oh yes you do, beloved. It is joy. David continued to say, " Thou hast turned for me my mourning into dancing: thou hast put off my sackcloth and girded me with gladness: To the end that *my* glory may sing praise to thee, and not be silent. Oh Lord my God, I will give thanks unto thee forever" (Ps. 30:11-12). There, let everyone that have breath praise the Lord and give thanks unto him for our weeping. This is so wonderful beloved! David prophesied that God will turn our mourning (weeping) into dancing (victory). And that our Father God will remove the sackcloth (oppression and lack) and girdeth us (embraced and consoled us) with gladness (joy). Hallelujah! David makes it clear because of this I will always give you thanks, I will not be silent (quiet). I will give thanks to you forever. You see beloved the same blessing is for you, the church and all of those who believe on the name of Jesus Christ, the Son of God. God is no respecter of persons, "For there is no respect of persons with God" (Rom. 2:11). O yes, "…weeping may endure for a night, but joy *cometh* in the morning"(Ps. 30:5).

TO THE FATHERS WHO ARE STRONG AND KNOWETH ME FROM THE BEGINNING, TO THE YOUNG MEN THAT ARE WAXING STRONG IN THE SPIRIT AND TO MY CHILDREN WHO ARE TENDER EVEN AT THE ROOT BUT RESILIENT AGAINST THE WICKED ONE , I AM THE LORD YOUR GOD WHO HATH CREATED YOU FOR MY PURPOSE AND MY GLORY, STAY STRONG IN MY SON JESUS THE CHRIST, TRUST HIM TO THE END, YOUR WEEPING SEASON IS AT BAY, DO NOT TARRY TO GIVE ME ALL THE PRAISE AND GLORY AND THANKS THROUGH MY SON JESUS, JESUS IS YOUR JOY, HE WAITS FOR YOU TO GIVE ME THANKSGIVING- I SAY DO NOT TARRY, YOUR JOY IS JESUS. JESUS IS THE KEY. "I Jesus have sent mine angel to testify unto you these things in the churches. I am the root *and* the offspring of David, *and* the bright and morning star" (Rev. 22:16). Amen.

Chapter Twenty-Seven:
"Deep Calleth Unto Deep"

❦

"Deep calleth unto deep at the noise of thy waterspouts: all thy waves and thy billows are gone over me" (Ps. 42:7). How marvelous is this beloved! Oh how we love this scripture, we bless his holy name, dearest Jesus. We bless our Lord Jesus because he is the one who saved us. Jesus is the one who delivered us from our adversaries. Jesus is the one who kept us safe from all harm. When one surrenders their life to the Lord there is a letting go that one does by the Spirit. When we surrender our life to our heavenly Father, and God, we did this, no doubt, through our Lord and Savior Jesus Christ. It was Christ that helped us to surrender. There is no way we could have possibly surrendered without our heavenly Father pulling us back to him by his power. "No man can come to me, accept the Father which hath sent me draw him: and I will raise him up at the last day" (John 6:44).

Oh yes beloved, calling us back to him. The Lord only calls his own; you must believe it, "Deep calleth unto deep" (Ps. 42:7). You see above we said the Lord calls his own. Do you actually believe our Father and God will call anyone except his own? Do you remember our Lord's prayer to our heavenly Father in the garden of Gethsemane? "And now, O Father, glorify thou me with thine ownself with the glory which I had with thee before the world was. I have manifested thy name unto the men which thou gavest me out of the world: thine they were, and thou gavest them me; and they have kept thy word" (John 17:5-6). You see beloved, Jesus makes it very clear… "thine they were and thou gavest them me" (John 17:5). Oh beloved, our Lord uses the past tense, "thine they were". You have a perfect understanding what our Lord Jesus Christ is speaking to you. Oh yes beloved, "Deep calleth the deep" (Ps. 42:7). Our Father and God are calling you back to himself. You will hear this all your days in your spirit, "Deep calleth unto deep" (Ps. 42:7). This is what the Lord is speaking to his servants, and all of those who believe on the word that his servant speaks for him.

Jesus continued to pray in the garden of Gethsemane. "Neither pray I for these alone, but for them also which shall believe on me through their word" (Ps. 17:20). This beloved, would be preaching the glorious gospel. You say God's servants have a lot of clout? Well, beloved, there is no person, not one soul, even God's precious servants who did not come to him by the glorious gospel of Jesus Christ. You must believe this. Now there is no need for jealousy. You see, when it is all over and done we will all be one glorious happy family. This is God's way!

Jesus continued to say, "That they all may be one; as thou, Father, *art* in me, and I in thee, that they also may be one in us: that the world may believe that thou hast sent me. And the glory which thou gavest me I have given them; that they may be one, even as we are one: I in them, and thou in me, that they may be made perfect in one; and that the world may know that thou hast sent me, and hast loved them, as thou hast loved me" (John 17:21-23). This is the glorious aftermath, "Deep calleth unto deep" (Ps. 42:7).

The Lord is calling you back. You say I have surrendered as the Lord hath spoken above. You say I have been in ministry for all of my life. You say I have been saved ever since I can remember; surely, the Lord is not calling me! Oh yes, he is beloved, "Deep calleth unto deep" (Ps. 42:7). You must understand, once and for all, God, our heavenly Father is pouring his heart to you. God and our Father know his own. Every parent knows their own children. It does not matter how long you say you have been saved or how long you have had a ministry. Are you truly in love with your creator? Are you willing to lose everything or give up everything just for Jesus? Are you? If he would come back today, are you willing to leave this world and return back to where you originated from? Do you see this situation or place we live in as foreign like our forefather Abraham? "By faith Abraham, when he was called to go out into a place which he should after receive for an inheritance, obeyed; and he went out, not knowing whither he went. By faith he sojourned in the land of promise, as *in* a strange country, dwelling in tabernacles with Isaac and Jacob, the heirs with him of the same promise: For he looked for a city which hath foundations whose builder and maker *is* God. Through faith also Sara herself received strength to conceive seed, and was delivered of a child when she was past age, because she judged him faithful who hath promised. Therefore sprang there even of one, in him as good as dead, *so many* as the stars of the sky in multitude, in as the sand which is by the seashore innumerable. These all died in faith, not having received the promises, but having seen them afar off, and were persuaded of *them*, and embraced *them*, and confessed that they were strangers and pilgrims on the earth. For they that say such things declare plainly that they seek a country. And truly, if they have been mindful of that *country* from whence they came out, they might have had opportunity to have returned. But now they desire a better *country*, that is, an heavenly: wherefore God is not ashamed to be called their God: for he hath prepared for them a city" (Heb. 11:8-16).

Isn't this just wonderful how our Father left a perfect example of how it should be?

Above it was said "And truly, if they have been mindful of that *country* from whence they came out, they might have had opportunity to have returned" (Heb. 11:15). There you see what our heavenly Father is revealing to you is that if our forefathers have been mindful of that country (the place where they left) they would have went back to where the promise of God was not. Instead they focused on the new place, a better place, heaven, home. "But now they desire a better *country*, that is, an heavenly: wherefore God is not ashamed to be called their God..." (Heb. 11:16). There it is, you see. This is a foundation for us. We are never to desire or love this present world. If we do we will put to shame our heavenly Father. "Deep calleth unto deep..." (Ps. 42:7).

Our heavenly Father has prepared a wonderful place for us. Our forefathers in faith knew this, do not you know it? Oh yes, you remember, heaven. "Deep calleth unto deep..." (Ps. 42:7). God is calling you back to himself. He always starts with our calling initially. Above when we said, "By faith Abraham, when he was called to go out into a place which he should after receive for an inheritance, obeyed; and he went out, not knowing whither he went "(Heb. 11:8). By faith Abraham when he was called... (Heb. 11:8) God initially called Abraham. "Deep calleth unto deep... (Ps.

42:7). God is calling you back to how it was from the beginning. You say, I do not remember. Oh beloved, it shall all come back to you. "Deep calleth unto deep... (Ps. 42:7).

DEAR CHILDREN, FOR I AM THE LORD YOUR GOD, FATHER OF THE UNIVERSE, I AM OMNIPOTENT GREAT IN POWER AND MIGHT, ALL OF THESE SAYINGS ARE FOR YOU THROUGH MY SON JESUS, COME BACK TO ME, NOT THROUGH YOUR MINISTRIES, NOT THROUGH YOUR SERMONS, COME BACK TO ME AS MY CHILD, JUST ME AND YOU FOR I LONG TO HAVE FELLOWSHIP WITH YOU, COME BACK, I AM THE DEEP AND YOU ARE THE DEEP-DEEP CALLETH UNTO DEEP, AT THE NOISE OF THY WATER SPOUTS ALL THY WAVES AND THY BILLOWS ARE GONE OVER ME, MY SON JESUS REMEMBERED HOW I DID NOT WANT BURNT SACRIFICES OR BULLOCKS FOR I HAVE ALREADY PREPARED ME A BODY, NOW I ASK OF YOU THE SAME, GIVE ME YOUR BODY, ALL OF YOU AS A LIVING SACRIFICE UNTO ME, HOLY AND ACCEPTABLE UNTO ME, FOR THIS IS WHAT I REQUIRE OF YOU, WE LONG FOR YOU, WE HAVE MADE PREPARATIONS TO REUNITE AS ONE, DEEP CALLETH UNTO DEEP: "In my Father's house are many mansions: if *it were* not *so,* I would have told you. I go to prepare a place for you. And if I go and prepare a place for you, I will come again, and receive you unto myself; that were I am, *there* ye may be also. And whither I go ye know, and the way you know. (John 14:2-4). Amen.

About the Author

Helen Trower was born in Cape Charles, Virginia in 1961. Helen now resides in southeastern Pennsylvania with her husband of 28 years. They have one daughter named Constance.

Helen is a servant of God and Jesus Christ. She preaches and teaches the gospel. God has called her out of the local church to have her own ministry, called Helen Trower Ministries, Inc., launched in 2003. God has given her a prophetic voice for all nations.

Helen's hope is to reconcile men back to God and to restore their hearts and bring healing to God's people through his Son Jesus Christ. During Helen's leisure time, she enjoys reading, writing, cooking gourmet cuisines for her family and friends, collecting and restoring antiques, playing croquet, evening strolls with her husband, Kent, and spending time at the ocean.